# THE SIX-STEP
# SPIRITUAL HEALING
# PROTOCOL
## CALLING FORTH YOUR
## HEALTH AND WHOLENESS

Rev. Robbins S.Hopkins, Ed.D.

**BALBOA.**
PRESS

A DIVISION OF HAY HOUSE

Balboa Press books may be ordered through booksellers or by contacting:

Balboa Press
A Division of Hay House
1663 Liberty Drive
Bloomington, IN 47403
www.balboapress.com
1 (877) 407-4847

Print information available on the last page.

ISBN: 978-1-5043-7443-9 (sc)
ISBN: 978-1-5043-7445-3 (hc)
ISBN: 978-1-5043-7444-6 (e)

Library of Congress Control Number: 2017901887

Balboa Press rev. date: 05/16/2017

# CONTENTS

For my beloved husband,
our cherished children,
and our loving parents.

# FOREWORD

I first met Robbins in 1969. Although the arc of a life's journey is always clearer in retrospect, the seeds for this book were evident in her worldview even then. She has made a career of living at the boundary between the known and the unknown, starting with her move overseas and immersion in another culture as a teenager. She then spent two decades researching cross-cultural adaptation and training others to engage more effectively with these unknowns. She went on to a successful career as a management consultant in international development.

Twenty-five years ago, confronted with healing challenges of her own and in our family, she went beyond the improvement of communications across the known world to communications in the spiritual realm. She keeps braiding new threads with the old, as you will see from her chapter on "global healing" where she has continued to integrate her international and outward-looking perspective into her spiritual work.

She describes herself as an ordinary mystic. I have always understood "ordinary" in this context to mean she is grounded in daily life - in ordinary time. In most other respects she is anything but ordinary. She is, however, eternally practical, even in her approach to calling forth spiritual healing. She takes an empirical approach and constantly tests her methods, reads the research, and collects feedback from her clients. She is a fan of things that work and the healing protocols she shares in this book are seasoned with years of experience helping clients.

Her prose is rich and we are rewarded with deeper nuances when we take the time to meditate on the meaning. She clearly does not expect anyone to absorb the book in one reading. Indeed, a major reason she finally sat down to write it was to provide her colleagues and clients a reference to all the learnings that have shaped her journey so these lessons and techniques can be shared more broadly.

In this book, she sets out specific and practical methods for us to clear the fears and imbalances that keep us from embracing our whole selves. She has refined these methods after years of working with clients and deep meditation. She has gathered this wisdom into a Six-Step Spiritual Healing Protocol.

One of things I admire most about Robbins is her courage. This is not to say that she is fearless, but that she faces her fears over and over, clears them from her field, and moves beyond them. I have come to appreciate that this is a rare form of courage indeed.

One of my favorite bits of wisdom that she shared with me early in her journey is the idea that we get as many chances as we need in this life to clear whatever we have come here to clear. It was only later I came to understand that depending on whether we have the courage to face our fears, the repeating nature of these opportunities may be the good news or may be the bad news.

As her partner on the journey and one of the primary beneficiaries of Robbins' evolving understanding of spiritual healing, I am deeply pleased to see this book come to fruition. It's time that a broader community of seekers experiences the transformational power of what she has learned.

In our relationship I am the tender of the hearth where the flame is sometimes low but radiant among the shadows. Robbins is the one who lights the lantern and holds it up and out into the darkness. The flame is bright and the darkness does not overcome it. May her book be a lantern for you in the darkness and may the sacred flame burn brightly for you and in you.

Giles Hopkins

# CHAPTER ONE

# Introduction

I AM AN ORDINARY MYSTIC. My life has been squarely set in the ebb and flow of human life and at the same time, I have pursued years of meditation and spiritual work with the Divine Realm. Because of this dual existence, I have chosen to stay in this world rather than to withdraw to a convent or a mountaintop. In this book I share how I continue to expand my work with The Divine Oneness in the midst of my daily life.

I first began writing and teaching about spiritual healing in 1995. However I was called to spiritual topics as early as 1956. As my healing experiences grew, I felt a call to share the processes revealed to me in Silence. These processes can help us clear our unhealed energies and address the imbalances they create in our bodies and energy fields. I have worked with a range of imbalances manifesting as chronic pain, failed relationships, addiction, depression, grief, boredom, blocked arteries, apathy, migraines, anger, self-hate, anxiety, mental disabilities, insomnia, feeling unsafe, irritations, tension, infections, dislike of self, cancer, obesity, and others.

All human imbalances can be traced back to blocked emotional, mental, spiritual, and self-protective energies. Further, these blocked energies cause imbalances in our societies, institutions, governments, economies, religions, natural environment as well as our bodies.

For millennia, we have come to earth in bodies and imagined that what we saw was all there was. In fact, what we are seeing, experiencing, and feeling in body is only a small part of who we really are and an even smaller part of All That Is. The vastness of All That Is extends beyond our physical in-body sensing capabilities. We have to become very still and quiet to sense what is beyond our own bodies, feelings, thoughts, and experiences.

We need to listen to our inner selves, our own deep knowing, in order to "hear" beyond our ears, to "see" beyond our eyes, and to "know" beyond our tangible experiences. As we become quiet and peaceful, we learn to experience Divine Presence wherever we are. Before consciously seeking Divine Presence, we may have had experiences with the Divine. The conscious seeking of connection with the Divine Presence means we can connect whenever we want to, not just when the conditions line up perfectly. The longer we consciously seek this relationship and stay on an intentional spiritual path, the more doorways open to Divine Energy.

Our major religions typically teach about God, Divine Presence, The Oneness, or All That Is. However, every person needs personal experiences with the Divine to develop trust and confidence in All That Is. Religions provide general pathways to connection with Divine energy. Every religion endeavors to point in the general direction of Wholeness/God. Individual inner exploration and seeking though provides a lasting, deeply satisfying personal relationship with the Divine.

Some people need just one experience in their life to open the channels with the Divine. Others need regular, consistent experiences with the Divine to really know that Divine energy exists within and all around them.

Mystics spend the core of our lives consciously seeking a relationship with God. We spend months and years pursuing our human relationship with The Great Oneness. At some point, we begin to understand how anyone can do this efficiently and successfully.

My experience has been a journey of increasing awe, amazing revelation, and powerful transformation. I do not recall wishing to be a mystic when I was growing up. Indeed I probably had no idea of what a mystic was. Even now, I do not for the most part fit the stereotypes of a mystic. I am married, have two children and a daughter-in-law, live in an extended family household and have worked all my adult life in the ordinary flow of daily life. In spite of this outward pattern of my life, my inward journey has been that of a mystic. I love all that is revealed about eternal truths, Divine power, infinite love and unbounded knowing. For many years, I could simply never get enough quality time with all things Divine.

I was most fortunate to have spent seven years in intentional Silence, five to eight hours daily, before going about my daily work, greeting my family and sharing our lives together. Though those patterns of intense seeking have altered over the years, the profound Presence of God is the most central characteristic of my life. This relationship continues to inform and transform my life every single day.

This book has been created in partnership with Divine Beings and their shared wisdom. I had been working with Divine Beings as my partners for many years before undertaking this book. We first worked together as I did my personal inner work of clearing away old feeling and thoughts that no longer served me. Then we worked in partnership to help others do their inner work. Now we have continued in partnership to write about how this spiritual healing process brings wholeness in body, mind, and spirit.

This book is about how to intentionally grow an intensely personal relationship with Divine Presence to bring you balance, health, joy, and peace through expanding your own deep well of love.

## USING THIS BOOK

There are numerous ways to use this book. You can read straight through the next sections that deal with motivations to meditate, stories about healing, insights about how to expand consciousness, and ways to get ready to consciously connect with the Greater Whole/God/All That Is.

Perhaps though, you have already passed through these topics on your own journey. You might be interested in trying out the healing protocols or casting out negative spirits or learning about how to stop carrying other people's pain or sorrow. Use the Table of Contents as a guide to find where you want to begin.

You can also use this book as a teaching guide for yourself. You can learn to clear your blocked energies and command them out even before reading about the journeys and insights shared here. If that is your calling, go for it. I would suggest you begin with Chapter Seven with the Six-Step Spiritual Healing Protocol. This chapter will get you started. It also has an extensive section of frequently asked questions and answers.

When you have some experience with the Six-Step Protocol and other healing approaches, you might return to read about personal insights other seekers have received through their journeys to inner peace and balance. In other words, this could be a reference book for you. Look at the Table of Contents and go where you feel you are led to start.

You may be someone who is motivated by exploring things you have never heard about. If so, begin at the end of this book in either Chapter Eleven, Advanced Healing Interventions, or Chapter Fourteen, Global Healing. You might then work backwards to pick up needed information if you want to explore specific healing steps for yourself.

Alternatively, you might be seeking support for healing work you are already doing. Chapter Eight, Working with Divine Healing Entities, may be your perfect place to begin this book. In that section, you will be introduced to amazing groups of Divine Beings each with specialties and talents who are committed to supporting human beings during our journeys here.

Eventually though, do consider calling in healing for yourself. Every time you clear blocked energy, your consciousness rises. This is the amazing truth about inner healing and clearing. Every time you clear away old anger, fear or resentment, your consciousness rises. In other words, you get closer to Divine Presence.

I used to calibrate my own consciousness using a hypothetic scale of 1-1000 with 1 being the lowest consciousness possible in human body and 1000 being the highest consciousness possible for humans. David R. Hawkins, MD, further explains this technique in *Power vs. Force.*[1] I calibrated this for myself in order to come to the absolute knowing that every time I cast out blocked energies, my consciousness rose. That was a huge motivator for me. I was a most skeptical ordinary mystic who lived in the show me realm for years.

If you know how to use kinesiology, you may delight in testing your own level of consciousness as you begin this process. Whether you measure your consciousness level or not, as you clear blocked energies, your consciousness rises. It is impossible to slide back into a lower level of consciousness once a higher level is attained.

Even when faced with persistent, disturbing imbalances, which seem intractable, you can't slide back in overall consciousness. Once you have moved to a specific level of knowing you can't mess up and lose the level of consciousness you have reached.

At times, you may feel you are back to the beginning or that you are deeply stuck. However, a sufficient determination to clear old stuck energies again and again, until they are really gone, is the path forward.

Every moment you invest in working on your own issues, brings a greater conscious knowing of your eternal connection with Divine Presence/All That Is. This brings lasting peace to you individually and to us collectively. It is worth every ounce of effort you put into spiritual healing for yourself and for our planet.

Peruse the Table of Contents and dip into parts of the book until you find your interest piqued. Begin there. Then choose something else that appeals to you. You can also read this book straight through as written. Anyway you proceed, you will receive that which is meant for you.

## THE LANGUAGE OF THIS BOOK

I have chosen to capitalize all references to Divine Energy. That includes the following references to God, All That Is, Divine Source, Spirit, Divine Grace, Perfected Love, Great Oneness, Yahweh, Unified Field, Allah, Elohim, Great Spirit, Sacred Space, Quantum Space, etc. I also capitalize all references to types of Divine Beings including Angels, Archangels, Divine Light Workers, Ascended Masters, Divine Healing Entities of Highest Light, Cosmic Light Beings of the Universe, Nature Intelligences, Devas, etc. The capitalization indicates that the energy we are speaking about is Divine.

This energy can be called by many names all over the world. Regardless of the specific terms used and by whom, the principles of interaction for healing with all Divine Energies are exactly the same. The different terms used for Divine Energy and Beings are intended to be inclusive for all people. The ways shared here to effectively connect and work with Divine Presence for healing apply to all Divine Beings and all Divine Source energy.

Use whatever terms work for you and substitute your own terms where those you use are not specifically named. The principles of connection and communication, healing and rebalancing specified in this book apply to all human and Divine Energy regardless of what we name it.

All the cases used in this book are derived from personal experiences I have had with individuals or groups. All names and identifying characteristics have been changed to protect the personal history of these people or groups. Further, there are times when a composite case has been formed from different individuals working with the same issue. In the few cases when a person might even suspect a case could be theirs, their permission has been granted to use the example as written even though their names and circumstances have been changed. All that is shared here has come from personal inner work and from working with others along their journeys unless specifically footnoted.

## AUTHENTIC PRAYER AND MEDITATION

This book is about authentic prayer, powerful beyond all limits. The most powerful, authentic prayer has to be based on the universal spiritual principles of Love and Wholeness. Every human being is made in the image of Divine Love. Additionally, our eternal souls are Divine Energy in human form, having a human experience.

You are here to learn, forgive, and heal from past hurts, traumas, and bad choices made in times while being in body. You are here to celebrate the joy of all life. God is within and you are always able to connect with that Divine Knowing, if you persistently seek this connection in your life with all your focus, energy, and determination.

At your very core or spirit, you are made of the same flame as the Great I AM/God/ All That Is. You are made in the image of All That Is. As a Divine Being in human form, you have free will. You can either embrace or totally ignore your Divine roots in every part of your life. Whatever you give your power to grows. You are the only one who can create Peace and Balance in your life.

Everyone arrives in this dimension with accumulated emotional, mental, spiritual, and self-protective baggage that manifests in your body, mind, relationships, affairs, and your soul. You can accumulate as much baggage as you agree to take on or you can command out this baggage that does not serve you well. Unloading this baggage is at the heart of authentic prayer.

When working with authentic prayer, you pray knowing you are already one with God while seeking to set down feelings, thoughts, fears, and anxieties that you carry at the conscious, sub-conscious, unconscious, and supra-conscious level, your soul level. Every time you lighten your load by commanding out blocked energy, your conscious knowing of God expands. You become consciously closer to Divine Light, Love and Wholeness.

Prayers spoken from a place of separation from All That Is/God are inherently weakened, as they are not set in the universal principles of the Great I AM. Much of what you may have learned about prayer may not be serving you well.

For example, supplication at its fundamental level is about asking for something from another. This book is about commanding and calling forth Love, Healing, Peace, Forgiveness, Grace, Creativity, Balance, and Wholeness from the core source of your being. Your being is always connected to the Greater Whole, even when you feel profoundly lost, hopelessly depressed or irreconcilably ill. There are lifetimes of learning within this book for the taking. So, where do you begin?

One place to begin is in Silence. When you quiet your mind, you are able to hear the still small voice within. Most of the time, extroverts spend time in communications and interactions with others. For introverts, much of their time is spent in their minds working through life experiences. Silence though is helpful for all people, regardless of your orientation to others. You may just differ from another in how you seek Silence and in what works for you.

Meditation is the conscious seeking of Peace and Balance. For many, meditation connotes sitting in a room, breathing and thinking of nothing. That is one way to experience meditation. However, there are many types of meditation: walking, moving, dancing, standing, creating, sitting, gardening, swimming, biking, and lying meditation, among others. Some people swim expressly to quiet their minds and experience inner peace. Others bike and can feel their connection to the Great Beyond. Some people ride horses and feel taken beyond this dimension to the expanded world beyond. Those drawn to create and perform music can at times touch to their inner connection with Divine Source.

Each type of meditation has characteristics that can help you touch to inner Peace and Balance and to your knowing of Divine Source. Each experience of intentional Silence can be a doorway into your own spiritual growth. You have to be the one to do the exploring, to want to experience inner Peace and Balance. That is your part of the equation. All else is given.

Make a choice to consciously seek the energy of Divine Connection. It is waiting for you just as close to you as your breath. You are already wired for Divine Peace and Balance. You just have some remaining work to release yourself from thoughts, feelings, and fears that keep you from your own True Self.

Meditation efforts are always challenging in the beginning. Your mind has a life of its own and runs amok a great deal of the time. You have to tame your thoughts and feelings by regular and disciplined effort to spend time in Peace, Centeredness and Balance.

This book touches lightly on meditation and to a great degree, assumes that you have some way to consciously seek Silence. Healing and insight come from inner seeking. If you are looking for real Peace and Balance, you will be open to seeing where you are separate from the states of balance within yourself. This book is devoted to helping you discover what is not serving you well because it separates you from Balance, Peace, Grace, and Ease. Authentic prayer and meditation opens you to a world of infinite possibility.

# CHAPTER TWO

# Invitation to Seek

THE MOST PRECIOUS GIFT YOU HAVE is your ability to connect with Divine Oneness. You are already hard-wired within to do this work. However, your human mind and actions often create real barriers to connecting with Divine Source. Being connected to the Oneness is like having a lifeline permanently and reliably present. You can have awareness of this connection or you can choose not to have any awareness of this connection at all. The choice is yours.

When you are not aware of a permanent human to Divine connection however, you live in greater fear and greater mistrust. This restricts some of the blessings you can receive because you have static on the line in the form of these feelings of fear and mistrust. Becoming aware of the Divine Presence opens a new set of energetic doorways you can pass through to receive help, support, guidance, healing, peace, and wholeness.

One of the most efficient ways to expand your consciousness and connect with Divine Love and Wholeness is to learn to love yourself, wholly and completely. Some have an easier time than others coming to a place of loving self-acceptance. Perhaps you have taken this trip numerous times through eternity and you can remember more quickly. Perhaps you have healed many major imbalances before this life and you therefore come in with fewer fears and concerns for yourself. Or perhaps, you have received specific spiritual help early in life due to the roles you have come to manifest in this lifetime.

Alternatively, you may feel prey to all the negativity, fear, mistrust, and anxiety around you without the means to perceive any other options. You may be confused and feel that your mind runs amok in all directions and preys on your vulnerability of feeling separated from Divine Presence.

Humans frequently believe that energy varies from one to another based on the personality, beliefs, and form. This is not complete Truth. Humans profoundly differ from one another based primarily on their stages of consciousness and evolution of the soul.

Once there was only space. Then space expanded into infinite forms. The energy behind all form is the same energy. The energy behind all life is the same energy.

Today's view of life is flawed in great measure. As a soul seeker, you are given a unique form and circumstances from which to learn the soul lessons most needed to accomplish your mission while in body. However, you can spend lifetimes focused on the physical and material aspects of your life that are almost exclusively determined by your mind.

If the mind has power over the human being, then fear, guilt, shame, apathy, anger, grief, desire, and pride are prevalent. If the soul, and therefore the heart, has power and allegiance with the human being; then love, compassion, forgiveness, balance, grace, creativity, peace, and joy are prevalent.

Consciousness is the protector of society. As consciousness grows, society becomes safer. Consciousness is the awareness of Divine Presence within. There are a number of accepted myths held by western societies that are not Divine Truth. Becoming aware of these myths and their separation from Divine Truth helps us reexamine our actions and responses to fear and perceived danger.

Here are some of these societal myths:

1. Other individuals can stand in my way and keep me from getting my blessings and just rewards.
2. Hard work is the only way to reap the bountiful riches of a good life.
3. Success and prosperity are up to each individual's ingenuity and determination.
4. Life is a haphazard set of events, relationships, and experiences.
5. An individual must procure for him/herself all that is needed.
6. The power of the person lies in his/her ingenuity, determination to succeed, ideas, and actions.
7. Life is what you yourself make of it.

8. Success is where our material rewards are realized and recognized by others.
9. To succeed materially is why we are all here.
10. Fear is a marvelous motivator.

As you move through this book, these myths will be subjected to the spiritual truths of consciousness, love, and forgiveness. Some or all of these myths may be transformed by insights given about the deep truths that exist for all eternity. Perhaps some of what is stated in these myths is accurate in some situations but there is deeper Truth that holds for all beings, for all time, from all backgrounds, and for every situation.

The only lasting way you can achieve a meaningful life is through expanded consciousness. All other pursuits eventually are empty. No human can fulfill another human's needs fully. Only Divine Love can do that. Therefore, you are each in this life play to find your own way, help others along their way, and continue to seek the Truth.

Consciousness is the hope of our people. It is the only lasting way to Peace, Sustainable Living, Joy, Love, and Prosperity. The world is in chaos on many fronts and loving communion is most needed. Life is always growing and expanding, changing and reforming. The core of life however is Spirit. Therefore, you can spend lifetimes pursuing worldly passions and not feel happy, fulfilled, or healthy. Eventually all beings must come to a place where they must attend to the inner terrain. This growth of the inner being is nothing like that of the mind.

The journey to great consciousness is shrouded in energy veils and the seeker has to deeply desire Peace, Love, Joy, and being in the Presence of the Divine for these veils to lift. You can be successful in intentionally seeking the lifting of the veils and in seeking ways to clear your emotional, mental, and spiritual bodies of their many blocks and false thoughts. This is process I would like to help you develop for use in expanding your consciousness.

## TAKING YOUR OWN JOURNEY

Life is a series of events to which you give meaning. The way you give meaning to each event is affected by how you see the world, your opinions, and your perceptions. In other words, you assign meaning to your life experiences as a result of your thoughts and feelings. You create your own world by the way you assign meaning to the events in your life. Two people can have the same experiences and due to the way they assign meaning, they can have very different reactions to the exact same experiences.

Success in life comes from your feelings about yourself. No outward manifestation of wealth or success can give you a deeply successful sense of your own self. Many people live as if there is another very tantalizing TV channel running along side their home channel, broadcasting millions of outward reasons for their being here. If you find yourself totally focused on the accumulation of material wealth, influence, power, or success in the outer world, you may indeed be out of balance by neglecting your home channel. You may be pursuing all the wrong goals in search of happiness, health, peace, and balance.

The only lasting sense of satisfaction comes from spiritual growth. You know that has happened when you can look back in time and see your emotional progress. Spiritual growth has happened when you can think of what was painful in the past and not feel the sting of pain in the present. You know there has been progress when you can look ahead to something that has bothered you in the past and feel no anxiety about what you will face.

How do you get to this place of balance, peace, and self-satisfaction? Spend time in Silence connecting to All That Is/ Divine Presence/ Perfected Love naming and releasing your fears and negative feelings in exchange for more Divine Light and Presence in your human mind. It sounds straightforward. However, there are very few places to learn to effectively accomplish this because this process is fully experiential.

When you first begin to seek conscious Silence, you can start by simply noticing where the mind takes you. When you become aware of a thought, you let the thought go and return to the focus on the breath. You can say "breathe in, breathe out" as you settle into Silence to help you stay focused on the present.

Your mind will be very active in the beginning. You may work here for weeks or months before you can get the mind to fully quiet down. Each day though, especially in consciously opened Sacred Space, you make progress. (For more on Sacred Space, see the first part of the Six-Step Spiritual Healing Protocol in Chapter Seven.) Keep showing up in

Silence with the intention to connect with the Greater Whole within you and surrounding you.

All the books in the world can't substitute for the act of consciously selecting Silence and opening to Divine Oneness. You can be an accomplished scholar of sacred texts and still only have a mental knowing of the scripture. The sacred text, and all texts, this book included, can only point you in the direction of seeking. The journey has to be taken up by each individual.

It is easier to undertake such a journey with a sacred person of Divine Wisdom. However, in the West, generally, we do not have a tradition of seeking in this way. You might consider joining a meditation group or opening Sacred Space by asking to join with meditators of the Highest Light around the globe to enable you to more easily enter into Silence. You have to begin the journey in whatever way you can and consciously trust that you will receive all the help you need along the way. For indeed, you will. I began my journey into Silence by sitting with my back to a large walnut tree. That tree was my companion in the Silence.

Often seekers begin their journey into Silence through reading, meditating, taking workshops, or journaling. Seekers can begin an inner journey by exploring options, ways of thinking, and ways of doing inner work and healing. This process of entering Silence is akin to bearing one's soul before another person. To do that, you have to implicitly trust that other person.

To enter into Sacred Silence, to seek Divine connection, you have to come to peace within, about your concepts of God/Great Spirit/ Divine Love. You need to establish trust with the Divine on your own terms. This usually requires some sort of search for books and teachings that speak Truth to you. Ideas, teachings, theories, help move you from where you are to where you want to be. You need to seek experiences of wisdom precisely because they can gently lead you to a deeper knowing of yourself and of the Divine Presence. Other people's experiences can help you develop the curiosity and courage to take your own leap into Silence.

The vast majority of human beings define God/The Great Oneness/ Elohim in human terms, with human frailties, motivations, and characteristics. Most humans greatly limit our concepts of God because we primarily use our minds to define All That Is/Alaha. I have been frequently reminded, that I must regularly seek communion with Divine Wholeness/ Perfected Love while in Silence, to begin to touch to the expansive nature of the Divine.

Ultimately, you must pursue some form of Sacred Silence with All That Is/Divine Presence/God in order to grow in trust, insight, peace, and balance. When you arrive at a point of trust that you will be safe while seeking and that you will be shown your true loving self, extraordinary things can be accomplished.

In taking that step into Silence, you need to "unzip" from all your roles of mother, father, daughter, son, teacher, sales executive, trusted friend, celebrity, doctor, cook, entrepreneur, tech wiz, etc. The act of unzipping from all you think you are is a powerful first step in and of itself. The unzipping begins a process of setting down the roles you carry, the responsibilities you hold, the worries you have, and the expectations you have of self and others. You unzip from these roles because they provide a very limited definition of who you truly are.

## THROUGH PAIN TO GRACE: PART OF MY STORY

I grew up riding bikes every day to and from the train station where I took a train to school. I rode bikes all year long in all weather. I played soccer and volleyball before it was common for girls in the US to play these sports. I kayaked regularly on a river, ran in the woods, ice-skated on canals in the winter, played kick the can, and capture the flag. I was very physically active. I lived in The Netherlands from ages 13 to 17. The outdoors was a delight to me. Fast forward a few years and I continued biking, hiking, swimming, dancing, and playing tennis through and after college. I felt my life was very happy, active, and filled with love of movement and physical activity.

In my twenties, I began to have back pain both in my upper and lower back that stayed with me constantly, for 19 years. In that time, I was mostly restricted to walking when I was not in pain. I did walk three to four miles on good days and could occasionally bike but there were many weeks that I could do neither. I was rear-ended by a utility van that totaled my car and put me in a neck brace for months. I saw dozens of health practitioners: osteopaths, chiropractors, orthopedic surgeons, physical therapists, talk therapists, manual therapists, sports medical practitioners, acupuncturists, pain specialists, energy healers, biofeedback specialists, massage therapists, and cranial sacral specialists over my 19 years of back pain.

My life was focused on going to healers at least two or three times every week. The pain continued with no apparent physical reason that anyone could find, with one exception. An osteopath told me that none of the muscles in my back could hold my bones in balance. Thus began years of injections into the tissues in my back. At one point, I was putting myself in traction everyday to try and rid my body of pain.

I was committed to finding a way out of the pain. Yet, at the same time, there was a point when I realized that I had lost all hope that I would ever be really pain free. It happened gradually but one day I became aware that I had not felt I could be pain free for years. This shocked me, saddened me, and brought me to deeply question what my body was trying to say to me that I was not hearing.

I had spent years and years looking outside myself for healing and wholeness. With every new practitioner I saw, I felt hopeful until that experience did not really offer lasting healing either.

I eventually learned to meditate, took yoga, and learned to be still within. I became a Reiki Master and for two years I did lying meditation with my body every day while it healed. I began to understand that healing happens within our being and is not brought to us by others outside of ourselves, though there are certainly helpful therapies to aid us along the way.

As I began to go within, seeking balance and peace with myself and with those around me, I did slowly heal and reclaim my body and my life. This book is in part about that process. I am sharing what I continue to learning about clearing blocked energies, speaking truth to myself, commanding out old feelings and thoughts that do not serve me, and being still in Sacred Silence.

## CONSCIOUSNESS CAN TRANSFORM YOUR LIFE

Consciousness is the process of becoming fully aware of your inner thoughts and feelings. In the process of becoming masters of these thoughts and feelings, you begin to experience Peace and Balance in every aspect of your life. When you engage in a full exploration of consciousness, you discover that you are really returning to your own True Self. Your True

Self is loving, kind, thoughtful, wholly integrated, fully balanced, and One with All That Is. All else that you may have experienced is being shaped by your thoughts and feelings that can often be completely separated from who you truly are. Your thoughts and feelings are humanly created and therefore, necessarily limited.

Consciousness is the power that every person is seeking. You may spend years looking hither and yon, far and wide. However, for the most part you do not look inside. The process of looking inside is not normally taught in our educational institutions, through few of our seminaries, and in almost none of our medical schools.

Where can you really learn about seeking God within? Why would you take on this task, unless there was great emotional or physical upheaval? Even when you do eventually seek connection with the Divine, while dealing with physical and emotional challenges, the process seems tinged with fear and sadness due to the significant imbalances.

These negative emotions though are not due specifically to the seeking of connection with God/All That Is/Allah. Rather, the heaviness is due the imbalances you are dealing with in the outward realities of your life. These times though often get confused and labeled as: I can't meditate, I don't like to be quiet, I don't know what I believe regarding Spirit, and I have no connection with All That Is.

Consciousness is the process of coming to a place of Peace and Balance while being in body. For the most part, those in body do not know about Peace and Balance while in body. Those in body spend countless lifetimes looking for Peace and Balance in the outer world, the material world. There are endless dramas that can fully occupy us for numbers of lifetimes where we are engaged with daily life but disengaged with Divine Presence, Peace, and Balance. Therefore, we need to connect with energy where a deep wellspring of Knowing is present. We need to connect in order to discover what leads us towards Inner Peace and what keeps us from Inner Peace.

Every human being has a human mind, human body, and an eternal spirit. When you come into body, you immediately come into contact with a race of individuals who are experiencing fears and doubts most of the time. Even if you were wonderfully connected to Spirit before coming into body, when you enter into this dimension, you usually take on the energy of those around you. The most powerful characteristics of this energy are fear and doubt.

All discord of any kind has its roots in fear. Fear is the absence of Love. Thus, as you take on more and more fear during your short years here, you literally block the energy of Love you were created in and may have lived in, in other dimensions. You begin to experience increasing discord in your life unless you find some way to connect with Divine Energy.

Overwhelming discord, fear or imbalance are the conditions that usually spur a person to seek Divine Connection/Divine Peace. You have experienced some mental, emotional or physical discord. The focus of this book is how to bring about a personal connection with the Divine so that it positively affects your daily life. In other words, how do you connect to and activate your internal connection with the Divine?

Before you can actually trust the concept of Divine Presence, you need to know what that concept, energy, and Presence encompasses. Many of our old and often unspoken views of God as the kindly man in the sky, the father who gives you what you ask for, or the loving being who will always make you feel better, are wholly inadequate because these views are greatly limited and personified due to our human minds.

Most of us have made an image of God in terms of our own limited "person-ness." God is an energetic Presence that is All That Is. How do you wrap your mind around that? The short answer is, you don't.

You have to experience this Presence to know it. Our minds cannot know the full extent of God or Source Energy. However, a first step can be exploring the qualities of the Unified Field.

According to Deepak Chopra, this list below of 25 qualities of the Unified Field was developed and agreed upon by a group of physicists. Maharishi Mahesh Yogi, the founder of the Transcendental Meditation technique, gathered these physicists to describe the Unified Field/God/All That Is.[2] This set of qualities that they agreed upon may help you realize the vastness of the Unified Field/God Presence.

Though this following list of Divine qualities is exquisitely specific and expansive, these are still only words that capture a thought to which a specific vibration is connected. In order to personally know these qualities or attributes, you need to enter into Sacred Space and experience the vibrational presence of All That Is. This list of qualities of the Divine can help you open your personal barriers and boundaries as you explore ways of connecting to I AM energy.

The 25 qualities of the Unified Field are:

1. Total potential of natural law
2. Infinite organizing power
3. Fully awake within itself
4. Infinite correlation
5. Perfect orderliness
6. Infinite dynamism
7. Infinite creativity
8. Pure knowledge
9. Unboundedness
10. Perfect balance
11. Self-sufficiency
12. All possibilities
13. Infinite silence
14. Harmonizing
15. Evolutionary
16. Self-referral
17. Invincibility
18. Immortality
19. Unmanifest
20. Nourishing
21. Integrating
22. Simplicity
23. Purifying
24. Freedom
25. Bliss

A fuller explanation of each quality can be found in, *Creating Affluence: The A to Z Steps to a Richer Life* by Deepak Chopra, chapter 4. [3]

# CHAPTER THREE

# Conscious Connecting with All That Is

THREE IDEAS ARE FUNDAMENTAL to your development of an understanding of healing and to calling it forth on your journey to wholeness. These are holding love, facing discord and surrendering. Each is addressed in this chapter.

## HOLDING LOVE

When you think of God/The Unified Field/All That Is, the concept of Love is often used to describe the general concepts you are trying to connect with. When Love is upon you, the world seems with you. When you feel separated from Love, you are mostly miserable. So the question arises, how do you invite and hold Love in your daily life? All the outward ways of finding and keeping love are usually talking about love with a little "l". There are thousands of books on getting the right love for you, keeping the love you have, attracting others to love, loving self in order to love others, loving your children, loving your mother, your father, or your siblings, loving your animals, etc. For the most part, these books focus on the outward seeking of love, securing love, attracting it, having love, fostering love, manifesting it, or creating love. In other words these how to books are designed to help you "get love".

You are encouraged through story, prose, history or poetry to be a certain way, say certain things, look a certain way, act a certain way, and think a certain way in order to "get love". Many of these self-help books or love stories explore what this process does and doesn't look like in one's daily life.

One major thing missing however in this search is that you cannot find other humans who can fully meet your vast and expanding need for Love.

You have to go to the Source for full, whole, balanced, and unconditional Eternal Love. You have to go within to reconnect with All That Is/God. That is the only place you can find an eternal, magnificent, expanding, unconditional, balanced Love. This type of Love is present everywhere. It is all powerful and all knowing. This Love supersedes all other types of love because it is the source of all forms of love everywhere on the planet.

This Source Love is the most powerful force in the Universe. It brought The Oneness into being. The Oneness is that from which all comes and to which all returns. The Oneness and All That Is are one and the same. Each and every being, place, or thing is of the Oneness. However, the vast majority of human beings are unaware of being a part of a larger Whole.

You may have touched to Divine Oneness, through some life experience. However, Angels and Ascended Masters from all traditions have repeatedly reminded me that as humans, we are generally unaware of the most magnificent, beautiful, powerful, exquisite, explosive nature of the Source Love. This magnificence is inherent in each and every being, place, and thing within the Universe. As you are learning more about the nature of Divine Source Energy in body, so on the other side, all Divine Beings continue their journey eternally towards greater and greater communion with The Oneness. Every time you are in body, you have the opportunity to clear all blocked energies you carry from this and previous lifetimes that keep you feeling separated from Divine Source Energy.

What would it look like if you decided to remedy this general state of unawareness? How might you begin to explore the larger terrain of Love? Where would you go to learn about Love?

The only place I have ever found that you can infinitely learn about Love is within intentional Silence. Within the Silence, you discover both the Presence of All That Is and the individual knowing of the Oneness that each and every person has within. Every single one of us is of the Oneness. The Oneness is just that, the deep experiential knowing that we are all from the same Source. We were all created in Love, by Love, for Love regardless of how our external lives, skin, words, deeds, hair, cultures, religions, or thoughts appear in our body and our lives.

There is no other place to learn these lessons because the teacher has to be the Oneness itself, the Presence of All That Is. Almost every human lacks a full knowing of Divine Love. There may be a few in body at this time, capable of this knowing and there have been a handful of others through out the centuries. For most of us however, we need to go within and seek the Inner Guide to help us experience The Presence.

Teachers are still needed to help provide a road map of consciousness. Teachers can to help you understand the signs and messages along the journey and see the roadblocks you have set up along the path. The teachings themselves have to flow ultimately from the Oneness, from All That Is. Until you have repeat experiences with The Presence of God, all else is like looking at an incomplete masterpiece. The masterpiece has the potential for completion but there it sits, unfinished, un-whole and therefore out of balance at given points in time.

Until you enter into The Presence, you can endlessly seek that ultimate fountain of Love and Oneness. You can look over, under, around, and through life with your five senses. You can earnestly look without a deep and lasting sense of fulfillment. You can spend lifetimes searching for Divine Peace, Divine Love, and Divine Joy. These qualities can never be lastingly found in the dimensions of daily life unless you experience the Knowing of Divine Oneness. With this knowing, everything in life is possible. Even that for which you have repeatedly searched in daily life without finding it becomes possible and can finally be experienced through a personal experience with The Presence of All That Is.

These delightful possibilities are only words. If you want to really experience The Presence as you read, take a few minutes out, put down the book, open to the Divine Oneness/God/Divine Love, and simply ask for the experience of The Presence in your life. "*Come, Divine Oneness, come consciously into my life.*" Sit in Silence and wait until you feel something shifting within. Do this often in search of this connection.

It is self loving to remember that you may need to do this many times before you can truly sense vibrational energy beyond yourself. All the blocked energies in your mind and energy field keep you from having an immediate open channel. However, showing up with the intention to connect is the first step to being able to manifest a deeply felt connection with Divine Source Energy.

As you wait upon the Oneness, you will learn to slow down, release your fears, expand your senses and receive this new vibration perhaps for the first time or once again after a long time. Each time you sit and open to this vibration of The Presence, you will come closer and closer to really sensing this within your being. You may have a number of blocks or stuck energy in the beginning and so you may initially only be able to know what Silence is like. The more Silence you seek, the more Peace you will receive over time.

Every person is wired for seeking the Presence. You have a fervent desire to reawaken to All That Is. This is because of the deep love of the Divine Beings for each of you. They know without a shadow of a doubt that when the Knowing of All That Is becomes accessible and conscious, you are then able to experience more Joy, Peace, and Balance in your daily life.

You come wired for the Divine Energy of Oneness but you also come with the free will to have any life you desire for yourself. Therefore, if you choose to carry anger, remain in fear, seek darkness or operate in disingenuous ways, you experience a life that is a reflection of these choices you have made. If you choose to have a life that is conciliatory, forgiving, generous and in integrity, you will experience a different life that comes as a reaction to these different choices.

As you are 100% energy, you act in accordance with and are affected by the principles of energy in every aspect of your life. As you sow, so shall you reap, as the proverb says. Energy is charged with certain vibrations. So, you can charge the energy you send out with love and all its attributes or you can charge the energy with fear and anger and all those attributes. You will receive back an energetic reaction that is attracted to and compatible with the energy you send out. So, if you desire a peaceful, harmonious life of joy and balance, you need to do everything you can to send out energy that is full of love and forgiveness. This enables you to receive back a life filled with experiences that resonate with your own love vibrations.

The challenge is that we often do not realize what we are sending out or why. What is it that an individual does that indicates that they are operating from fear, or shame, or guilt? What does this look like in real life? What does a life look like that is sending out love, forgiveness, appreciation, respect, and cooperation?

These realities are the reason that intentionally expanding consciousness is perhaps the most important action you can take for your health and happiness, and for that of your fellow Earth-mates. Without actively seeking an expanded consciousness that is in essence a more vibrant relationship with God, we simply continue to make the same mistakes in our thoughts and feelings, lifetime after lifetime.

## FACING DISCORD

The early warnings of discord come softly. Perhaps the warning is a disagreement with a minimum of emotional content. Perhaps the warnings come as a difference of opinion or different reactions to the same, shared experience. These are the beginning signs of discord. If these experiences are processed, reflected upon, and understood then escalation of these issues has no need to reoccur. If however, these situations are not considered, then these same issues are likely to repeat and replay sometimes with the same person and sometimes with different persons, but around the same issues.

Why is it that we have repeating areas of conflict, heartbreak, or discord throughout our lives? Why do we continue to draw some of the same difficult interactions over and over again? This is because we are all energy beings.

If you have a huge issue with something, you put out compromised energy whenever you face that issue in your daily life. You attract to yourself the very issues you are most sensitive to. This is so that you will stop, pay attention, and release that which is causing you pain and anguish. How else could you know what is not whole, what is out of alignment with Peace and the Oneness of All That Is?

Your energy attracts and uses life experiences to call you to a greater understanding and awareness of where you are putting your attention. Each conflict is substance for clarifying the human thoughts, feeling, and actions that are not of Divine Light/God and that originate within your little or human self. If at first you don't attend to these calls, you are given other chances. If you have not attended to these issues for a very long time, the situations become increasingly charged and may even result in physical deterioration and imbalances of a very serious nature.

Joanna was in her 40's when she came to see me. She was a recovering "anger-holic". Her colleagues had told her repeatedly that she needed support and help because she was always flying off the handle over some issue or another at work. This had been feedback given for a long time, in many situations. She reported being very unhappy in her previous work environment as well as unhappy with herself for never being able to control her anger towards others.

Joanna presented energy that was delightful. She had a beaming smile and twinkling eyes. To me, this indicates the intention to connect with others even if this was not effectively happening in her life at the moment. After months of group and individual meditation and reflection on all sorts of emotional issues, she said one day, "I think I am actually growing spiritually". Then without warning, her old abusive self showed up and she lambasted an assistant in a public setting while she was "making herself" give a party she did not want to give. All the while, knowing she was losing it and still completely unable to stop the tirade towards this other person.

She came for meditation after this incident, greatly distressed with herself. She was deeply troubled that she had acted this way and she was completely stumped as to what had actually triggered all of this. She was determined to find the core reason for this outburst because she was ashamed of her actions and did not want to have this happen again.

After some inner searching, she determined that she was deeply afraid of having to do something she did not want to do in order to make a living. This rang true to her as she had carried this energy for several years. Joanna had been out of work for a year, and was considering returning to work, so this deep fear simply erupted without her even realizing what was "working her". She had not wanted to give the party she agreed to give and found herself resenting everything about the situation. Therefore, she erupted. This time though, she named the fears involved, agreed to release that energy during prayer, and all that old fear energy left her body for good.

Looking at this with a longer perspective, Joanna had carried resentment, fear and anger for years about having to work in a negative environment, in order to make a living. The year's respite from doing this did not heal the energy though because those feelings of fear and anger were still present within. When she began to consider returning to work, she was still afraid that she might again have to do things she did not want to do. She was still angry and fearful about what that might mean.

When she was next doing something she resented, explosive anger came barreling out of her, even distressing her more than before. She was now aware of what she was doing. This time though, she knew to look within herself for the explanation of her behavior.

In Sacred Space, she called forth the healing she needed. She cast out all her fear of having to do things she did not want to do. She called in the energy of Balance and Peace. She eventually felt real Peace and Balance. She was able to forgive herself. She was able to set down the resentment and fear of having to do something she did not want to do. She was also able to apologize.

This is a good example of what can be accomplished by using the Six-Step Spiritual Healing Protocol explained in Chapter Seven.

## SURRENDERING

Life is full of chances for our surrender. Indeed surrender could be seen as the major activity of our entire being. For as you surrender to God/Perfect Love/Wholeness, and thereby to your highest or True Self, all that you have held onto that is not serving you well, can leave you. With that surrendering act, you can then experience the Divine version of Love and Grace, which you may not have even known was possible.

Surrender, however, is a greatly misunderstood concept. In human terms, it brings up all kinds of connotations of the loser, giving up, throwing in the towel, being the weaker of the pair, being run over, being walked on, etc. All these definitions of surrender however, come from the human concepts of power, which create some of our most persistent dramas in human life.

If you embrace your human concepts of power as the "haves" and the "have-nots", surrender has to be defined through those same power terms as well. Essentially, in such a mindset, if you surrender, you are failing, you are giving up, you are less than, somehow. If you surrender in this context, you become one of the "have-nots".

However, if you understand that surrender to God is letting go of control, bad choices, unsupportive situations for a better reality than the one you presently have, the connotations about surrender are completely different. You can begin to imagine that surrendering can bring more abundance, more joy, more peace, and more balance. Surrender to Divine Oneness though still requires trust in the Divine Energy you are working with. It also requires, enough trust in your own goodness that you can let go of what is not serving you in the present, before you know the full results of what your life might be, after surrender.

All too often though you simply tighten the noose around what is known and familiar, because to let go and make a different choice is deeply scary. When you have huge upheavals before you, you need to have taken a lot of small steps in the direction of letting go and surrendering. Then when big, challenging issues are facing you, you can make the leap to surrendering to Divine Providence and Presence.

## CHAPTER FOUR

# Communicating with Divine Source

YOU MAY COMMUNICATE WITH SOURCE/God/Divine Presence through unfocused wishing, anger, pleading, bargaining, or you may have no way to communicate at all. There are, however, some simple ways to communicate with Divine Presence that seem to work better than others.

## SUCCESS WITH DIVINE COMMUNICATIONS

Releasing old assumptions about how to connect with God is a good place to start, because whole new ways to feel connected to Divine Energy and Love can then show up. Above all, you have to be in your heart space when you talk with God/All That Is. That means that no amount of prepared text will actually enable you to effectively speak with God yourself.

If you write a prayer before saying that prayer, you still need to speak the prayer from your heart and not from your head or from the paper upon which it is written. When you are seeking connection with Divine Source Energy, you need to be with God in the moment and not in another time and space as, for example, might result from using a prepared prayer.

Preparing prayer or using others prayers may help you prepare for your encounter by enabling you to clearly say what is on your mind and in your heart. However, the best and simplest way to speak from the heart before God is to simply say what you are thinking. There is no one else present judging what you are saying. You are the only judge present and so you have to focus on speaking from the heart, from that part of your deepest self that is already one with God. You may not feel you are one with God but you are and part of your being knows this beyond your mind.

Pleading, unfocused wishing, and bargaining do not work with Divine

Oneness very effectively because these ways of speaking assume that something is missing in your life or in the lives of others. There is nothing actually missing. You may not be receiving what is all around you, Divine Love, Joy, Blessings and Balance. However, the deep truth is that all that is needed is provided. When you are not receiving all that is needed, there is simply a disconnect between you and Divine Presence, which you have most probably inadvertently created or carried with you from previous soul experiences. Your part of the connection has been lost but the good news is, you are exactly the one to bring about the reconnection!

As a human, you may look at something and think, "This is missing in my life and needs to be corrected". This is not fully accurate. We are exactly where we need to be on our journeys. What is more accurately happening is that undesirable circumstances are manifesting in your life because you feel disconnected from God. This is due to a false sense of separation. This is a myth we as humans continue to give our power to over and over again - the myth that we are not connected with Divine Source.

If you were not feeling separation from God, there would be no trauma energies active in your current situation. Most of us don't have a trusting, powerful, fully activated and vibrant connection with God. If though, all that is needed is provided, how do we experience or receive all that is provided? What is keeping us from receiving that powerful, all present, all knowing Presence in our lives?

To know this, you have to go within and ask. Where am I separated from Divine Source/God? Where am I causing static on the line, reinforcing fear or succumbing to doubt about my relationship with Spirit? What exactly is in my way, keeping me from a full and vibrant relationship with God?

When you do not experience a deep connection with The Greater Whole, you are often experiencing energy that is manifesting as pain, loss, anger, hopelessness, loneliness, illness, depression, boredom, guilt, shame, addiction, etc. When you are not manifesting a balanced, whole, vibrant relationship with All That Is/Divine Universe/God, you are often focused on your humanly perceived lacks and imbalances of all kinds. When you have pain and disease, these feelings only exacerbate your sense of disconnection and imbalance.

A basic law of the Divine Universe is that what you focus on grows. When you focus on your perceived lacks, they grow and multiply. This happens when you give your human power to a feeling, thought, or action. The additional charged energy and focus enables that emotion or action to grow. You give it more energy and it grows bigger. By doing this, you set up a highly charged environment within your own being that attracts other emotions of a similar low vibration.

If you think you are being taken advantage of, that feeling grows and grows because you are giving your life energy to that fear condition on a daily basis. More experiences of this kind come your way because you have prepared the energetic space for that feeling to thrive. As long as the fear remains in your feeling self, the imbalances will manifest, even if you dearly want them to go away. Wanting imbalances and unpleasant situations to go away is insufficient though, to have them go away. You have to discern the underlying reasons for your negativity and command those out of your energy field. You have to change the focus of your energy to enable balance to be restored to your life.

Focusing on the dark is the opposite of focusing on the Light, the Divine, or the Universal Goodness. If you are focusing on the things in part of your life where you are unhappy or angry, you keep experiencing imbalance after imbalance. These imbalances can include such things as loss of job, increasing discord, illness, accidents, infections, personal losses, failed relationships, poor sleep cycle, depression, among others.

All discord and negativity thrives in an environment characterized by a felt separation from the Presence of God. Where there is a felt separation between you and Divine Love, there is the real possibility of human suffering.

The existence of pain and suffering in your life is wholly within your hands. Whatever you positively envision and hold to with Divine Energy, will come to you. It may not be in the exact form that you have envisioned or in the exact way or time you have envisioned it, but it will come.

This is because of the Divine Law "Ask, and it shall be given you; seek, and you shall find; knock, and it shall be opened unto you". (Matthew 7:7, King James Bible) This law is how the entire Universe is set up. Live your life in this way and you will have results compatible with your soul's desire. Your soul is the part of you that is of Divine Oneness/ God. Your soul is eternal and is your own True Self, as well. So, that which is in your eternal best interest is what you will receive when you know deeply that you are One with All That Is.

Prayer is one way to actively seek a personal relationship with God/Divine Source. When you pray, Divine Source, All Knowing Energy of the Universe notes your energy change and responds to that new energy. When you pray from your deepest Self, that part which is wholly of Divine Source, you alert both your inner being and the Divine Universe of this desire for change. The connection made between you and that Divine Energy is what brings about change.

You may think you have made a really great connection and still not be able to actually receive the blessings available to you. This could be because in general you desire new patterns and yet, you return to your old patterns for making choices regarding yourself and others. Then, you are in jeopardy of not receiving the desired blessings because you have returned to old patterns causing "static on the line" or because there is more old energy that still needs clearing. Old patterns take time to set down. If you keep trying, the old patterns will eventually go. Un-cleared blocked energies can keep you feeling disconnected from All That Is until all imbalances around the specific issues you are addressing are cleared.

On the other hand, if you follow up such a prayer request with daily Silence in which you look within and ask to be shown where you are separated from God regarding the request you have made, you can clear the decks. You have a much greater chance of receiving the Divine Energy called forth because you are continuing to clear the pathway to Spirit. If you want change, all the conditions need to be present for you to experience that change.

## RAE'S JOURNEY

Here is a case of how seeking within can work in daily life. This process may seem messy when you are in the midst of it. Sometimes the next steps seem useless or futile. Often you cannot see the progress being made. Stay focused on seeking Peace and Balance, and you will be shown the way. This case demonstrates how someone might persistently seek Peace and Balance through inner work and learn to let go of ineffective feelings and stuck patterns.

*Rae desperately wanted peace in her home. She was worn out by the fighting and anger present just about every day, with those in her home. She was at odds with her husband over how much time he spent with her. She was holding the line with her oldest son around the mess he lived in on a regular basis. She was constantly getting angry with her younger son because of his tendency to loose or misplace his belongings. She was always feeling angry, taken for granted and overwhelmed by both working and keeping the house running. This usually blew up around dinnertime, when she began to cook dinner for everyone with no one at home to help. The "no help" was usually a result of her husband and her older son being at work and her younger son being at after school activities or needing to study when he came home late from school.*

*Rae blew up regularly when someone did come home while she was in the kitchen alone, getting dinner ready. That of course had the opposite of the desired effect as that person typically left the kitchen and did not reappear to help even if they were in the house.*

*One evening after months of this pattern, she simply went to her office and did not fix dinner. She stewed and stewed in the office but kept her determination and did not fix dinner for her family. This did indeed cause some attention to be focused on this event. However, the interaction was not positive because by the time the interaction happened with the family, everyone was hungry and she was very angry about months and months of this ineffective cycle. Her anger kept away any possibility of coming up with a better way to get the family dinner on the table.*

*Rae felt deeply troubled and quite angry by all of this. Further, there seemed to be no solution. After several sessions on this situation with Rae and after several months of meditation and Silence, there was a shift in family dinner preparation in Rea's home. However, she had to completely get rid of all resentment, anger, blame and judgment around this situation before a good solution presented itself for all family members.*

*Though she had wanted to have peace for months in her house, she needed to clear her emotional decks in order for that desire to come to fruition. She had to name the negative feelings she was focused on, ask for Spirit to lift those from her being and really let them go. In time, the entire situation healed itself.*

*She and her family worked out a varied plan to get dinner made with a minimum of hassle and time for both Rae and her family. The solution though necessitated clearing all the angry, gnarled energy that had surrounded this situation for months by everyone. The stagnant negative feelings had to be cast out of her energy field and those in her family so the right environment could be created, thus allowing the "waiting solution or goodness" to surface.*

You can live in any type of circumstances you choose. That can be in anger or peace, in fear or love, in discord or harmony. If you want a change in what you currently have, you have to begin with yourself to clear the emotional decks that are charged with your own negativity. Contrary to popular opinion, as adults, other people do not stand in your way, dictate your life, or keep you from living as you so desire. They can dictate some of the conditions and some of the aspects in which you live, but you do not need to let those conditions remain or choose discord as a way to respond to them.

If you however, join with Spirit and go into Silence and stillness, you can have the possibility of engaging with Divine Love to bring about changes in your life. The healing always begins with you. You have to stop choosing the negative, the dark, the anger, and the frustration if you want to have any hope of peace in your space.

You have to name those negative emotions within yourself and sit with Divine Presence in Silence until such time as you are really ready to let those negative emotions go from your luminous field. Then the solutions you desire can manifest in the new energy you have created. By off-loading negative energy you allow healthful conditions to emerge from the Bountiful Universe.

What does this really look like you might ask? How do you get from anger and frustration to peace and harmony? Here are excerpts from some interactions with Rae as she was slogging through her deeply held emotions.

**Rae:** *What I don't get is why do I always blow up especially when someone does finally come into the kitchen to help. I know that doesn't help one bit but I do it anyway, again and again.*

**Listener:** *How does it usually happen?*

*Rae:* Well, lots of ways. This week Todd began to set the table and I spoke up very clearly saying that I needed help getting the food on to cook because that's what takes the time. He said he didn't need the aggravation and left. I think my voice was pretty irritated.

Then, a couple of weeks ago, my husband came home early and offered to help. I was already way into the dinner prep so I gave him specific instructions about how to do the various things that needed attending to. After the third direction or so, he said he was perfectly capable of cooking the beans himself just fine and we got into a terrible argument over how to help when you come in late to the dinner preparations.

He was really angry and also, just left. I went after him and we yelled it out. It just makes me so upset to even recount all this. We really do love each other but put us in the kitchen at dinnertime and it's a danger zone.

*Listener:* What is behind the interactions, do you think?

*Rae:* Well, clearly anger. It just bursts out before I can catch it. I know, know, know the minute I blow that I am not helping at all. I'm like a machine set to self-destruct though, it comes out anyway and it seems to be more and more.

*Listener:* Right. I am asking though, what do you think is behind the anger? There are plenty of other households experiencing similar situations where the interactions don't get charged and negative. What is working you every time you are in the kitchen fixing dinner? What is fueling the deep anger you carry?

*Rae:* What do you mean? It is simply anger that I get no help, anger that no-one's around when I have to cook, and I end up having to do everything, anger that when I do get help, I blow it by being angry. It seems like an endless cycle.

*Listener:* Do you experience this in other areas of your family life?

*Rae:* Yes, just about every day there is something.

*Listener:* What other things trigger this response?

*Rae:* It could be my asking for help and getting a stall or an excuse. Yesterday, I told Jim to pick up his room for the 100<sup>th</sup> time, as it was a real pigsty. I am not usually very nice about it by the time I have asked him again and again. He blows up and says it is his room and if I don't like it get the "fuck" out. Real nice. Then, we get into it or I leave. Yesterday I left. But we still don't have a good solution to that, at all.

*Listener:* Yeah. Very hard, I'm sure. I am asking again, though, why do you think you get so angry with Jim over his room? Let's take a real extreme stance and say that he is right. It is his room. Why can't you let him simply pick it up when he wants to or not when he doesn't?

*Rae:* Well, then it eventually falls to me to clean it. Laura, our cleaner, won't touch the room unless it is picked up and I simply can't live with the mess week after week.

*Listener:* So, are there times that you go into the room and clean it up out of frustration?

*Rae:* Yes. After three weeks or so, I see red whenever I pass by the room.

*Listener:* So could it be that you get so angry because you are afraid that the responsibility will fall to you when he does not keep up his end? In fact, these responsibilities have indeed fallen to you several times?

*Rae:* Yes, I suppose.

*Listener:* If you didn't have the fear that it would fall to you, might you have an easier talk with Jim without it being charged? Can you see that perhaps happening if you had no fear you would have to pick up the pieces?

*Rae:* Yes. But I would not have necessarily thought of this as fear.

*Listener:* Let's look at the kitchen. Would you say that you are afraid that it is all on you with the kitchen as well? That everything is all up to you in the end? And that is where the anger is, really?

*Rae:* Yes. Well it is all on me and everyone feels that way clearly. I am so angry that no one helps and so it does all fall on me; the shopping, the planning, the cooking, and the yelling about it!

*Listener:* If you could be in the kitchen and be completely clear of all fear that it was all up to you, do you think you might react differently?

*Rae:* Yes. But I can't imagine getting there.

*Listener:* That is what we can take into prayer when you are ready to really let this go, this fear of having it all on you. It only takes a few minutes when you are ready to release this. We'll ask that all fear and anger energy around having the household issues fall on you, be lifted by Divine Source Energy. It will clear the emotional space within and you'll see more and more shifts at home.

Rae repeated this process over and over again in the following months with regard to all the issues where she was experiencing anger at home. Eventually her household was a more peaceful place. There were rarely angry words spoken. Her husband and children also learned to clear their fears behind their own anger. Eventually, even if anger was present it did not escalate to ugliness and discord. She said that she could never have released her many fears though without being in the Silence and without a connection with the Divine Presence, through that Silence.

This clearing and healing process is exactly what is presented in Chapter Seven, the Six-Step Spiritual Healing Protocol. It is designed to enable you to do your own healing especially with seemingly intractable or chronic situations and physical imbalances.

## CONNECTING WITH THE GREAT SPIRIT

The very best way I know of to consciously begin connecting with God is to enter into Silence. That may seem paradoxical but it is not really. Connecting with All That Is is usually a very subtle experience when we first begin though not always. Generally, the first challenge of the Silence is the realization that our minds have lives of their own and they constantly run with lists, concerns, thoughts, and plans. As the Divine Energy is invisible to most of us, being in consciously selected Silence calms us down.

It quiets us and allows our natural thought patterns to slow down, thereby bringing a sense of ease and relaxation. It takes a while until we experience something we can say is our connection with The Great Spirit.

The process of connecting differs for each person. Some folks experience colors; others see familiar forms like angels or cherubs in their mind's eye. Still others simply experience intensified vibration with no forms or pictures at all. All these and many other ways of experiencing The Great Spirit show up in meditation. Whatever happens for each person is totally perfect!

There are those who sit and immediately move into a state of suspended peace, totally unaware of themselves and those around them. There are others who move through different stages on their way to arriving at the state of meditation. Often the first step is the concentration or focusing stage. We may focus on breathing, say a mantra, recall a piece of scripture, recite a song lyric, or look into a candle flame. The act of focus enables our brain to slow down and allows our breathing to become even and measured. Whenever you sit consciously to connect with All That Is/ Divine Source, mediation has occurred. As you sit, more and more, you will naturally evolve to a deeper and more expansive sense of Peace.

Some people sit and others lie down when first beginning to consciously meditate. Other folks alternate given the day. Lying meditation is for inner healing and sitting meditation is for inner wisdom. Let your body lead you to what is most appropriate for a given time.[4]

You arrive at the fully bona fide state of meditation when you no longer sense the body, its boundaries, its location or the time. You simply have moved into The Great Oneness, Quantum Space, where All That Is, is present with each person.

This sometimes scares people. They don't want to let go of the driver's seat enough to go deeply into the Silence. They may fear they will not return. They may fear that they will have to face things about themselves they do not want to face. They may be struggling with to do lists, frustrations of the day or raw emotions while heading to meditation. However, total Silence is where you can finally connect with The Great Spirit/Holy Spirit/ Divine Love, in the most perfect way for you. In meditation space, you can begin to feel Love, Peace and a Connectedness that can never fade.

Nothing is required of you in order to connect except to show up with that intention. You have to show up, be still, ask for connection, and wait. Eventually, that connection comes and you begin to grow in learning what the various experiences and sensations mean.

When I first began serious meditation, I sat by a huge black walnut tree in Silence feeling vibrations. As that connection was established, I followed that sitting mediation with two years of lying meditation because I was in constant back pain when I began this journey. Now I most often sit or walk during my meditation times.

You may sit in a state of meditation and seemingly have nothing consciously follow you into present time, into your daily consciousness. You may have to sit for months before you begin to pick up on the subtleties of that communication and their meanings for you. This does not mean that the time is of no value, however. This does not mean that you are failing and can't do meditation.

Every time you sit with the intention of connecting you do indeed connect though it might not be in the way you had envisioned that connection. If you do not set aside time to connect with Spirit you are forfeiting a wonderful healing and supporting experience. When you show up with the intention of connecting, that is your time to receive love, supportive healing vibration, and Divine support from the Spirit of the Living God. However, that comes, it is perfect for the person and for the day.

Creating a conscious connection with Spirit is very much like creating a relationship with a friend. We have to show up or set aside time for the relationship to grow. This is exactly the same with Spirit/All That Is. If we do not set aside time that is wholly committed to being with Spirit, we lose the possible benefits from connecting with that wholly Pure and Loving Energy.

Many people meditate and then go about their day. When my meditation time is complete, I have chosen to explore this Sacred Space for healing. What follows meditation for me could be called contemplation or reflection. These times always lead to healing.

I usually reflect on what is not working well for me. What is causing my sense of disconnection or imbalance? This is a question I often think about as I am coming out of meditation. I then ask for and receive guidance and clarity around issues, persons or conditions that I am dealing with. This insight always refers to my energy and my imbalances regardless of how I am experiencing the imbalances. This is when I use the Six-Step Spiritual Healing Protocol presented in Chapter Seven of this book.

Another person's contemplation time though might be to simply hold a word or sacred verse in the heart while asking for further illumination as to it's meaning in his or her life. I also use time after meditation for expressing gratitude and appreciation for my blessings.

The bottom line is that Divine Source knows everything about you as well as you do, sometimes with more clarity. Your relationship with Divine Source therefore may be one of the only places where you can tell your truth and be totally accepted, warts and all. Divine Source energy is not a judging energy. You are the only one judging yourself in this relationship.

Being in Silence you can begin to speak your truth about how you feel, what you are dealing with and what you are concerned about. Though this is already known, you have the free will to pretend that Spirit does not exist and does not know the circumstances of your spiritual and human condition. You have all the time you need to bring your full self to a space of Divine Communion.

In order to grow spiritually, you have to tell the deep, complete truth in your relationship with God. Though, the Divine Oneness already knows the truth, your telling the truth is paramount to a successful relationship. If you try to fudge the truth, candy coat it, or adjust it, you will not be able to determine where you are truly separated from Spirit/Divine Peace/ Divine Abundance. You will simply stay exactly where you are. You have to actually raise issues and concerns you may have no idea how to heal or rebalance.

This is also true with any human relationship. If you build a relationship based on what you wish to be true rather than what is, you end up with either a stagnant relationship or no relationship at all.

As I ask the question about where I am disconnected with Divine Light, I am led further along that pathway while in reflection. I am the only one who can identify that which is not serving me well in my relationships, my life, my body, or my feelings. In the beginning, I found that I could not easily see what was not serving me well unless I spent time in that sacred energy of Oneness. I began to notice if I raised a general area of imbalance, the nature of my part in that imbalance got much clearer.

As you grow in consciousness, that which is not serving you well shows up for attention. You may be experiencing discomfort at home, anger with friends, discord with a spouse or failure at work. All of these daily experiences are signs of where you are separated from God/Divine Balance/ Grace in your thoughts or feelings. Your daily experiences become places of learning and potential sources of healing as long as you are connecting with Spirit. Otherwise, there is a great tendency to see your life as totally filled with suffering and difficulties.

This parallels any vibrant human relationship. At times in all relationships, you need to identify where you are separated from peace, joy, fulfillment, etc. If you don't name the issues, they remain and often fester. When you do not do the clearing of your own blocked energy with a relationship, one or the other person usually moves on, thinking that the issues are intractable, with no way to resolve them.

Release follows reflection and identification of where you know you are out of balance. It is essential to release those feeling and thoughts that are most separating you from God/ Divine Oneness. You are often given a place to begin your work when you first meditate. Wherever you begin your work is perfect. You are given all the chances you need to move into loving wholeness. If you don't get the message the first time, you are given many more messages over and over until you can't ignore these anymore. Unfortunately, many of us have to be facing a crisis to stop, be silent and connect with Spirit.

Releasing stuck and gnarled energy in Sacred Space frees you from repeating the same old unhealed fears and emotions. The stuck energy can leave your entire energy field. As you clear one area, others will surface. For example, as you clear old shame, you may be led to look at guilt, anger or pride that needs addressing as well. You will continue to be led to release feelings and thoughts that are not serving you well as long as you stay in connection and listen. This process is explicitly outlined in the Six-Step Spiritual Healing Protocol process described in Chapter Seven.

This process grows positive human relationships. If we simply fill up bags of negative issues with friends and loved ones and never let them go, they color every aspect of that relationship. We have to clear the decks of our old negative feelings and thoughts so that we can move on and embrace all that is inherently possible in the blessing of that relationship.

The very act of having an intentional relationship with Spirit is our choice, as is having a relationship with any human being. We can choose the relationship or not. We can choose to keep showing up with Spirit or with the human being or not. In both cases, the choice is ours. And in both cases there are consequences to deciding to forego a certain relationship. It is all up to us. We have free will given to us upon our birth into body. So, if you are making the choice for connection with Spirit, uncountable blessings await that choice.

Spirit is the greatest Counselor there is. Where else are all our full powers and wholeness known while at the same time, all the ways we are separated from Divine Peace also known? We are completely safe in this process because we can't ever be let down by God. Divine Presence is the Perfection we seek, the Peace we seek, the Balance and the Abundance we seek. This connection is one of eternal proportions. There is always more to identify and release of our human conditioning as we move more and more into Balance and into a place of Joy and Grace.

As each person grows in a Divine relationship, we begin to fully embrace the energy that we are One with All That Is even though we are not yet perfect in that Oneness. We come to a place where we begin to realize that God is both within and without and that realization is life transforming. Most amazingly, this process of intentionally seeking connection with Spirit experientially trains us in the most profound ways to build intentionally conscious relationships with humans in our lives as well.

The Great Spirit is all-knowing, all-powerful and everywhere present. Therefore, if we choose to develop a centered relationship with Spirit/ The Presence/All That Is, its blessings can extend to every corner of our lives; health, relationships, work, leisure, creativity, affairs, abundance, and family. We simply have to show up, tell the truth, identify the darkness, release that energy, and begin it all over again. We will become lighter, more balanced, more peaceful and with each step, more fully aware of our real power to create Love all around us.

# CHAPTER FIVE

# Foundations of the Healing Context

LET'S EXPLORE CREATING A HEALING CONTEXT. What foundational truths support rebalancing, spiritual growth, physical and emotional healing? Each person seemingly begins to seek alone, to test the waters, to read what others believe, to explore Silence, and to slowly consolidate spiritual learning. Spiritual learning is about getting to know your own True Self. You create your own healing context with the thoughts, insights, and truths that support your healing.

## PERSONAL REVELATIONS

There is an energy that is within and surrounding us that is greater than we can possibly imagine. Most of us live our lives without ever learning to use this energy, even though we are each Divine Beings having human experiences. Therefore, you can make the choice to live with conscious Divine connection or simply never make that conscious connection. You learn either way. I find though that living in partnership with Divine Presence is extraordinarily delightful. My rate of learning is accelerated and more effectively focused when I am conscious of Divine Presence in my life.

There are a few basic principles that help when considering living in conscious space with Divine Oneness. A fundamental learning for me was that I am eternally one with God/All That Is/ Divine Oneness even though I could not really feel it for a long time. I had hints that came repeatedly to me through conscious meditation in Silence. I could not fully grasp this however, before I had the actual experience of entering the void that I now call quantum space. I had entered that space time and again through Silence before I had a name for that space. In quantum space, for me, there were no thoughts such as we have as humans but there was amazing energy and I learned that all things are possible from that space within.

This is what I was headed for but did not know when I first consciously began my spiritual seeking. I began like most of us do, with some very challenging life experiences that sent me seriously exploring. For several years, I read everything I could get my hands on to expand my mind about the possibilities of connecting to Spirit/God/the Expanse. I was trying to figure out what made sense to me. I slowly began to find my way through the myriad of options in the greater world to what turned out to be my calling.

While absorbing hundreds of books, I also went to numerous workshops and seminars with vastly different groups and leaders. Along the way, I was ordained as an Inter-Faith Minister. I partook of both experiential learning and intellectual learning. I was very conscious of not really knowing what I was being called to do. I kept searching but I could not seem to get the clarity of purpose or direction I was seeking.

Seeking is another basic aspect of creating a healing context. We each seek uniquely. Our needs and souls truly guide us to what we need to face and release so that we can experience the Divine Presence in powerful and dynamic ways. I would even say that without the seeking, we are not likely to stumble onto a lighted pathway to Divine Knowing. It is in the seeking that we face ourselves, the darkness we carry, and the hidden perceptions we secretly hold about ourselves, and others.

When the outward seeking recedes, then we have the choice to begin the inner seeking through meditation and contemplation. This can be gradually eased into through journaling, reflecting on readings, listening to meditative music, or drumming. Eventually though, we have to enter the Silence regularly and repeatedly to absolutely know we are One with All That Is. No one can tell us this. We have to experience this for ourselves to own this Divine Knowing.

I began trying to meditate by sitting next to an old black walnut tree that came through the deck on our second story. I would wrap myself up in all sorts of warm clothes and simply sit next to tree's big trunk with my back resting against it. I felt a huge connection with that tree. When I was there I felt peaceful and still. The energy inside of me settled and I loved that special quiet time leaning against that tree. I realized that something wonderful was happening when one day I had spent quiet time outside with my tree and when I opened my eyes again, I was covered with snow. I had not felt a thing while in the deep quiet. I was exhilarated.

Alas though, that was not to be my central pathway into meditation. It was just a hint of what I might find, but sitting meditation was not my pathway. One of the huge challenges I had was chronic, seemingly unrelenting, back pain for 19 years. There were years of treatments, x-rays, shots, medicines, traction, heating and cooling pads, doctors, chiropractors, osteopaths and massage therapists. One of my major motivations for greater inner peace was to heal from debilitating back pain.

Part of my pathway was finding Reiki. I studied this healing process and eventually spent two years in lying meditation working on myself with Divine Presence to heal my body. I felt the most undeniably powerful physical sensations throughout my entire body every day I was in lying meditation. I began to know that I was connected with All That Is. I had never experienced anything like this before in my life. It felt like a line of high voltage energy moving through me. Many days I had to drag myself away from vibrational connection because I felt such Love in that space.

At this same time, I was writing letters to Divine Presence/God in my journals pouring out all my shortcomings, my fears, my uncertainty, my anger, rage, and lost feelings on a daily basis. The hours of lying meditation were like an elixir for my pain. This all went on daily for about two years. Then one day, I could not connect with that Divine healing vibration anymore through lying meditation. I lost the physical sensations of that connection.

I went into a dark soul space as I tried over and over to reenter meditative space by lying down and using Reiki energy on my body. There were six months of heart wrenching sadness, fear, frustration, sobbing, longing, debilitation, and stuck energies as I repeatedly tried to find the meditative space again. Lots of self-searching and self-recrimination followed each of these failed attempts at meditation. I was completely bereft. My connection with God had seemingly disappeared.

One day in bed trying to meditate, I was literally begging for what I was missing, to be shown to me. I slid out of my bed to the floor, with my head in my hands sobbing and my back to the side of the bed. Immediately, I felt the connection with Divine Energy again. I was so relieved. I was exuberant. I had felt so disconnected and frustrated. I had lost all hope of feeling connected again. As I sat there in that delicious Divine Presence, I realized that I was done with lying meditation. I was to experience sitting meditation now! I was reconnected and pointed in the right direction. I was filled with deep gratitude for this shift that enabled me to connect again with Divine Energy.

At the same time, I felt that my rate for "getting the picture" needed to vastly improve. I had continued doing the same things for six months and not once had I tried sitting meditation because I thought lying meditation was it for me. I could not believe that though I had felt so deeply lost, abandoned, and angry with myself that I had not once truly asked to be shown what I needed nor had I even once tried sitting meditation in all that time. What a learning this was for me and continues to shape the way I learn to this day. Now, I am always asking to be shown the way.

## UNIVERSAL SPIRITUAL TRUTHS

There has been extraordinary spiritual and personal learning shared with me along my path. One constant is that all individuals are already wired for Divine Presence. We are each and every one developed from Divine Light, Spirit and Substance. You may not manifest that connection consciously in this lifetime or you may choose to manifest that connection partially or fully. You have free will and you can live your life in the ways you choose.

Living your life without the benefit of connection with the Divine though, can be hard going. If you make that choice, you live your life typically feeling that your life is separated from Goodness and from Divine support. Frequently this choice manifests as energies coming from "it is all up to me" thinking. There are many humans living their lives this way.

Inner Peace would not usually be among the characteristics coming from these choices or this pathway. Inner Peace is something that must be consciously sought because it is within you and does not reside outside of you. So, though you are wired for God and Divine Presence, you may choose not to explore this connection for as many lifetimes as you want to live this way. The choice is yours.

There is usually some reason you begin to search for greater Peace and Balance in your life. It is rare that you simply have an ah-ha moment that seeking inner Peace could be good for you. Usually, you have some crisis or circumstance that leads you to seek within.

Another learning that is true for all humans is that part of your being is Eternal. You are each much larger than your physical body. Your body is a vessel for you to learn about your Infinite Wholeness. You are here for a short time in the expanse of all eternity. You have substance and experiences affecting you from the past. You will have others beyond this human life as well. You do not actually fade into oblivion upon death but rather change states as you pass from the current living body you have at the moment. However, the soul or the foundation of experience traveling with you continues through all of your forms or non-forms as you navigate Eternity.

Your Eternal Soul is constantly guiding you to greater and greater communion and Oneness with All That Is. Every single experience you have, the seemingly wonderful and the seemingly challenging, form your soul led process to help you connect with potentially fruitful situations. When you are connected with All That Is, you are able to fully manifest your own True Self. For at your core, you are Divine Material.

You may not feel like Divine Material in body for many lifetimes. Without seeking the Light within, you do not experience yourself as Divine Material. You can live your entire life feeling you are separate from God. You typically think you are here and God is somewhere else. You can only begin to know you are of the Light as you go within and connect with God energy beyond your mind, your body and your affairs. If you spend enough time doing this, you might get a glimpse of your real Power, Grace, and Light that is already within you. This Knowing grows as you expand the time you spend in Communion, Silence, and Stillness with All That Is.

Knowing God is not a mental process. Knowing God is an experiential process. There is no way to know God without experiencing God Energy in your life. You can know about God in a myriad of ways: reading, discussing, writing, musing, researching, speaking, serving, or advocating. All these activities help you know more about God.

Knowing Divine Source within yourself however, requires taking time out of your daily life and cultivating a seeking mind. "Ask, and it shall be given you; seek, and you shall find; knock, and it shall be opened unto you."(Matthew 7:7 New American Standard Bible) This extraordinarily powerful directive is true for all human beings.

You do not have to strive or achieve to be worthy of connection and communion with God. You, by your very existence, have this authority and right already. You do not have to be in any way "acceptable to society" to warrant the right or ability to connect to God within.

Your will and desires manifest greater Peace and Grace in your life. This is true regardless of any of the twisted messages you may have given your power to, along the way. All those imbalances in thinking and feeling can be re-balanced.

The desire for Peace, Love, Harmony, Balance, Hope, Grace, Forgiveness, Joy, and Oneness catapults you to expansive Source experiences. These experiences expand your inner knowing of All That Is/God/Spirit. This is Healing Grace manifesting.

## THE POWER WITHIN

We usually think of power as the energy to get something done, to influence, to control, to rule or to make something happen. What is often unconsciously assumed is that we are envisioning this power in our outer lives and as the world sees power. However, within each of us is Infinite Power, already. To access this, we have to come to a place of seeing ourselves in service to the Greater Whole. We have the power to access Infinite Possibility, Infinite Creativity, and Infinite Balance. All of these abilities are different types of power. The world is at our fingertips but the road to this power is within.

When you come to a place of knowing that you are truly of God substance, you begin to act for the goodness of yourself and others. As you begin to call forth healing for self and others, you start to tap into that inner power source. This inner power source is within you. Even more importantly, it is eternally connected to God Mind.

God Mind is All Knowing, All Powerful, and Everywhere Present. The spark that is eternally within you is also All Powerful, All Knowing, and Everywhere Present. However, if you are predisposed to use this power and energy for the detriment and harm of others in any way, you cannot access that Infinite Power. It is as if the veil comes down over this power source if darkness of any kind is your intention.

Further, if you are angry, full of rage, greedy, abusive, jealous, condemning, filled with guilt, hate or ruthless ambition, unforgiving, punishing, or judging, you will never tap into the power within. This power within only shows itself as you come to a place of wanting to manifest Peace and Balance within your own being. That is the doorway to the power within. The desire to be one with Divine Presence/The Source is the doorway to great contentment and inner power.

One client I worked with came with one of her interests to heal her relationship with her mother who had passed. The relationship had been tumultuous with a mixture of good and seemingly bad energy. This client, whom we will call Marsha, wanted to feel peace with her mother. She knew she carried lingering resentment, sadness and a deep sense of loss regarding her relationship with her mother.

We began with clearing her guilt, anger, judgment, worry and grief she carried in her own life with a number of other friends and family members. Her courage and determination brought her a place of peace that she could fully trust. There were months of work and eventually she reported that she was feeling much more peaceful, stable and happy. One day, she again raised the issues with her mother. It was time for that healing as she was clear enough in her own energy to bring this healing forth.

We called for her mother's energy to join ours in Sacred Space. I found that I was to be the voice for her mother's presence that day though I had never done that type of work before. Her mother spoke through me and she and Marsha completely reconciled their differences amidst much crying, laughing and smiles. It was a Holy time for all eternity and Marsha continued to process that for many months and apply that healing to many other situations and people in her present life, as well.

Touching to inner power manifests as speaking one's truth with Love, seeing the Light in others regardless of their behavior, setting loving boundaries, forgiving self and others, compassion with non-attachment, calling forth Divine Love, living in integrity, seeing infinite possibility as a world view and many other ways. When there has been enough clearing and letting go of your own human judgments, fears and self-protective energies, you come to a new sense of your own power, the power to set intentions and to have these manifest all around you.

The power within manifests in Divine timing. When you set down your hurts, grievances, un-forgiveness, pride, and rage, your own inner power manifests all around you in unimaginable ways. You are guided by your own soul through experiences in these lifetimes, to release all memories, feelings, thoughts, fears, and doubts that are not enriching you, in order for you to begin to seek the eternal power and balance within. This inner power is dormant until such time as you renounce the limiting human frailties, thoughts and feelings you carry. When you have cleared these untruths and imbalances, another set of eternal truths is revealed, about all beings. This encompasses the truth in every dimension that all beings are One with All That Is, including yourself. This is your very Divinely sparked nature whether you embrace that or not.

The power within has the capacity for infinite expansion unlike human power. Once you begin to work with your inner power, you can change and affect all things for the good. This capacity grows and grows as you move more deeply into a full knowing of God and quantum space. Quantum space in this context is the scientifically proven space from which all things manifest, and that in its resting state, appears as if nothing is present. Quantum space is God Space that presents as no form to the human eye. However, within this space is Infinite Possibility.

## THE CALL TO HEALING

Your current life is only a short stop along the continuum of your eternal existence. Therefore, what exactly are you doing here? You are here healing from your feelings, thoughts, fears, and doubts that you have taken on in body from this lifetime or another one as a result of your inaccurate sense of being separated from God. If you know you are one with God, you can see another's angry words as behaviors that are separate from the person him or herself. You may not like the behaviors at all but you see the exchange with benevolence for what has caused the anger and the lashing out.

You are called to healing by every single unpleasant experience you have in your life. Those beings put before you who raise discomfort, fear or rage within you are here to help you to heal, strangely enough through a Divine contract to work together in these ways. When else would you be motivated enough to ask what might I do about this interaction and my response to it?

One of the Ascended Masters, Jesus, taught the concept of turning the other cheek when attacked. An Ascended Master is a person who while in body comes to the full knowing of his or her Divinity and lives from that Knowing. There are Ascended Masters from all traditions.

How do you come to a place to offer the other cheek when attacked? Why this teaching? If we are all One having a human experience, then what is seemingly negative for you is really a call to healing. This applies to everything. If you are obsessed with your weight, or poverty, or stature or talents, these are all calls to healing. There is something behind these obsessions for you to learn from. If you carry deep sorrow, rage, jealousy or blame, this is also a call to healing.

You are called to turn the other cheek because the effective response to attack behavior is about you getting the message you need to hear yourself, not blaming the other person. The other person has his or her own life to live. You can only be responsible for your own actions and reactions, and learn from those. You need to figure out what you have to release, set down, or heal in order to move on. You have no knowledge as to what another person's pathway is, in this lifetime.

Calls for healing can also come from your own body. The pain or dysfunction of your body is yet another call to healing. The body's call for healing is a more commonly accepted idea than recognizing anger and sulking energy as calls to healing. You however, may have a very limited human vision of what your hurting body is really saying to you. Hurting bodies for many people often result in heading for the drugstore or the doctor. We go to treat the physical symptoms usually.

Less well understood is that the state of the physical body reflects the state of your energetic body in every single instance. Whether you are dealing with an aching knee, an unstable sacrum, a sinus infection, cataracts, bursitis, or cancer, there are always unseen energies in your energetic field directly affecting your physical body. This is also true for the presence of diabetes, high blood pressure, Parkinson's disease or Attention Deficit Disorder and many other imbalances as well.

We have a few accepted and successful examples of doing inner work as a healing path to physical addictions such as alcohol, overeating and gambling. Alcoholics Anonymous, Overeaters Anonymous and Gamblers Anonymous have all taken a spiritual approach to going within in order to really heal from addiction. This is because addiction though it manifests physically, originally stems from imbalances in our emotional, mental, thermal (self-protective) and spiritual bodies. If we heal these inner imbalances, which manifest physically, then the body can completely heal in most instances. Usually though, the body itself still needs to be supported and helped towards healing and balance. Even if you understand all about the original reasons for addictions and may have even healed them, the body itself also has to be specifically attended to for full healing to occur.

In other words, when you have a physical imbalance, you are clearly aware of the imbalance usually due to discomfort. If you seek in Silence to determine what blocked energies you are carrying manifesting as a sore right knee, you will be guided to what those might be. Of course, you have to have a meditative practice to hear or receive guidance in this way, but it is available to you if you make an effort to connect with the Divine Knowing that is within and surrounding you throughout the Universe.

One client I worked with was manifesting chronic headaches. She had had her eyes checked and her vision was fine. She often got these headaches at the end of the day. This had been going on for over two months. When we went into Silence and listened for blocked energy, I heard that she was carrying feelings of being overwhelmed and all related symptoms, one of which was chronic headaches. When we talked more about this, she said that a good colleague and friend had left her company where she worked and she was feeling loss both personally and professionally. She confirmed that she was generally feeling overwhelmed.

We cleared for the loss and overwhelmed blocked energy and her headaches began to recede. However, she also needed to change some habits in the afternoon to help keep her headaches from manifesting. Beginning at 3 pm she was to take at least one 10 minute walk every hour until she headed for home. During that time she was to consciously breath deeply and stretch her arms, rotate her head and shrug her shoulders. She was to increase her water intake also, forgo caffeine. While sitting in front of her computer, she was to open and close her mouth and stick out her tongue consciously to release tension. This two-fold strategy of clearing blocked energy and keeping tension out of her body, led her to headache-free days.

## LOVE AND FORGIVENESS

All healing is created through love. Love is the manifestation of Divine Order in the World. There is no situation that enough love cannot heal, here so wonderfully captured by Emmet Fox.

> *Love is by far the most important thing of all. It is the Golden Gate of Paradise. Pray for the understanding of love, and meditate upon it daily. It casts out fear. It is fulfilling of the Law. It covers a multitude of sins. Love is absolutely invincible.*

> *There is no difficulty that enough love will not conquer; no disease that enough love will not heal; no door that enough love will not open; no gulf that enough love will not bridge; no wall that enough love will not throw down; no sin that enough love will not redeem.*

> *It makes no difference how deeply seated may be the trouble, how hopeless the outlook, how muddled the tangle, how great the mistake; a sufficient realization of love will dissolve it and will dissolve it all. If only you could love enough, you would be the happiest and most powerful being in the world.*[5]

The question then becomes why don't you have access to a sufficient amount of love to respond to imbalances in all areas of your life? You carry blocked energies in the form of feelings, thoughts, self-protections, fears, and doubts that directly affect your ability to access copious amounts of love to heal issues and imbalances that you face. When love is covered over by the fear of appearing stupid or the suspicions that you are not worthy of recognition, or the thought that you don't deserve to be happy, these blocked energies drag on your energy fields. The love, which at your core is truly who you are, is not accessible if covered over by such blocked energies.

If you basically dislike and judge yourself, what you look like, how you act, what you are doing with your life, you will truly never get to the love that undergirds every part of you. It will remain buried primarily because you have not gone inside to work with your imbalances that would free up more self-love and forgiveness for self and others. This is a crucial part of free will. You can choose to live your life however you want to, with all the consequences associated with those choices. Frequently though, you make such choices without even the awareness that you are actually choosing to ignore major thoughts and feelings that would help you immensely if you would turn and face them.

Here comes forgiveness. It is the antidote to hardness with self. It is the answer to bad choices, poor communications, mean behaviors, and a host of other ugly interactions with self and others. It is always waiting to be called forth from our powerhouse of love and all related energies.

Forgiveness is really a type of love. It is incredibly powerful and transformational. It has been written about through all of time. If you do not forgive yourself for choices you regret or are ashamed of, you will not be able to forgive anyone else. This is a huge secret hidden from many. You can try to force yourself to forgive someone whom you really still want to punish or blame and it will never work.

Basically, if you try to force forgiveness, demand it of yourself or try to be nice as a form of offering forgiveness, it will never stick. Lasting, complete forgiveness only comes from Love. Also, until you forgive yourself for your part in the interaction totally and completely, you cannot forgive another. You may be able to play act forgiveness but it will not ring true because if you withhold forgiveness from yourself, you do not have it to offer to others.

A client came to work with me regarding her very challenging situation with her sister. From my client's perspective, she and her sister had a surface though civil relationship. This had been going on for over fifteen years when we began the work. At that time, they hardly ever talked but when they did, her sister would frequently rage at her on the phone and rarely apologize, as she reported. This often happened when her sister had been drinking. They did gather at family reunions and holidays, and everything on the surface was seemingly fine. The rift my client felt was still present though never acknowledged by her or by her sister. They carried on as though nothing was amiss. We began to work with her feelings and emotions concerning her sister. We cleared her anger, blame, and expectation energies she had about sister's behavior towards her.

After several weeks of working together, she shared that she had recalled a memory as if the event happened yesterday. She remembered a situation when she was a child, where she was railing to her parents how she wanted nothing to do with her sister and that she was always getting in the way and ruining her fun with her friends. Her younger sister was right there listening to every word. This recalled memory was truly her first sense that what she had done over and over again through their years together was to exclude her sister completely from her life with anger and judgment.

This scene from the past was a clue as to where her forgiveness work needed to begin. Over a series of months she worked on forgiveness of her part in the poor relationship she had with her sister. She then began to forgive her sister for her attitude and behaviors towards her. She said she was called over and over again, sometimes in the face of new very angry or hurtful behavior, to forgive her sister 70 times 7 times, unceasingly, so she reported. She said at times wanted to lash back at her, lecture her, shut her down and so, she had to remove herself from her presence to stay centered.

Then one day she reported with tears in her eyes that her relationship with her sister had healed fully and completely. They had had some real conversations both in person and on the phone and "I love you" began to be said again after more than 25 years. She simply said, "it really worked". This kind of healing and forgiveness awaits us all.

An added benefit if you forgive yourself, is that you thereafter carry the vibration of "forgiveness possibility" and that in and of itself affects all your interactions with others. Vibrations you carry signal who you truly are, in the world. It is impossible to succeed in faking forgiveness unless the persons we are faking it with do not know forgiveness for themselves. Then they might not spot the behavior for what it is.

On a broader level, if we are all One and we are all here learning, then forgiveness is the lubricant that makes interactions with others hum. You can forgive because you are learning like every other person in body. You forgive because it is an act of love to do so. You forgive because it raises your vibration and makes you feel a whole lot better.

## GRACE AND EASE

Another piece of the foundation for a Healing Context involves Grace and Ease. Grace and Ease refers to allowing. A state of allowing is a type of loving peace. When you put up any kind of resistance, your energies are in a combative state and therefore cannot be fully supported by universal Divine Energy that is completely based on love. If you work from a place of partnering with the Wholeness, you work within Divine Love and Power in the Universe. The saying "go with the flow" is a powerful spiritual stance. As you understand and accept that all that is happening is already in Divine Order for your growth and learning, you can more readily accept what you cannot change *and go after what you can change.* This is part of living with Grace and Ease.

You might wonder when you are very sick or feeling deep sadness, how can that be in Divine Order? We are all in exactly the place we need to be for healing, learning, forgiveness, and rebalancing. The overarching Divine Order is that when you come into body, you have chance after chance to learn what you need to learn in the exact situations you need to learn it. Ease and Grace can be the experiences you have, if you are listening. If you are not listening, you have to have more and more confrontational experiences until you have to listen to what you need to do to bring about the healing you are seeking.

In some cases, the healing you are seeking is not even conscious, so the process to get to it may be challenging and arduous. However, every experience you have is a potential learning for you until you complete that cycle, and become free from the imbalances you have attracted often unknowingly to yourself, for your own learning. In every situation you always have free will. Even if you see yourself as a victim, you are in charge of your own choices in whatever situations you find yourself.

Every time you push, you are creating resistance. Every action in the Universe creates a reaction! You can choose to accomplish things through pushing, attacking, lashing out, criticizing but there is always an equal, usually negative reaction to making this choice. Often the resistance takes the form of stress or tension for you or for others. Choosing Grace and Ease as a way of interacting does take practice, creativity, and determined effort. It is worth it though because whenever the loving choice is selected, you have the entire universe of Loving Wholeness working with you.

This is not to say that choosing civil disobedience or demonstrating against injustice cannot be effective. In some cases this is the only way the needed change can be brought about. Civil disobedience in the face of injustice can be incredibly powerful especially when no force or violence is chosen. Indeed,

Gandhi, may well have felt that civil disobedience was choosing Grace and Ease in the face of pervasive injustice. When there is a choice, choosing a method from a place of Grace to bring about change contains vastly more positives than physically pushing against injustice, darkness, pain, and sorrow. This is because the most powerful healing energy in the universe is Love. This is true for any individual and for all of us collectively. Violence, anger, and rage beget more violence, anger and rage. Choosing Grace for your own life challenges is the shortest way through the darkness.

## LIGHT VIBRATIONS

Another foundational aspect of a Healing Context is the nature of the world of vibrations in which we live. The whole world is made up of vibrations. Energy and its vibrations comprise everything we see and experience. Even parts of the body vibrate at particular levels. You can call Divine Healing Light in the form of vibration into any situation, space, body, animal, or plant. Light vibrations work on the resonance principle. A higher vibration raises a lower vibration through resonance. Thus, when you heal blocked energies within yourself or in conjunction with others, the vibration of the body or situation rises because you are working with Divine Light vibrations that are always higher than human vibrations. As you clear your fields of previously held low vibrational views, emotions and fears, the vibration in your body naturally rises.

Many of the vibrations we work with during spiritual healing, cannot be seen by the human eye. Your most personal experiences with Divine Presence present themselves through vibration and sensations and less frequently through human vision or sound. Some people on occasion have visions while in a meditative state, through dreams, or possibly while in a conscious awake state. Some people hear sounds, music, or words when in conscious Silence. For the most part though, when working in spiritual healing, we work in a world of unseen and unheard vibrations. As you progress through meditation and clearing, as your consciousness expands, you have increasingly more vibrational awareness of Divine Presence. It is often at these times that other forms of connection such as visions and sounds come into your energy field.

There is also an entire spectrum of Divine pure color rays that you can call upon for healing yourself or others. This is an example of one form of

Light healing. This information shared below comes from Archangel Ariel. There have been all sorts of attributes, qualities, and conditions shared from various beings tied to specific colors. However, this information is specifically for use as healing vibrations.

Here is a small sample of colors and their abilities to restore certain qualities in our lives. You might begin to work with these pure color rays as follows. While in conscious Sacred Healing Space, you can say, "*I call forth the Divine pure color ray of* [the color] for [name of imbalance]".

Here is a partial list offered by Archangel Ariel of specific colors and the healing qualities they bring forth.

| COLORS | QUALITIES |
|---|---|
| Pink | Unconditional Love |
| Red | Trust |
| Orange | Courage |
| Yellow | Illumination |
| Green | Forgiveness |
| Blue | Health |
| Indigo | Truth |
| Violet | Balance |
| Golden White | Communion |
| Warm White | Protection, Safety |
| Pure White | Joy, Happiness |

These color rays have the potential to bring healing energy of a specific nature to imbalances in your body, relationships, and affairs. However, before you are able to fully take these pure color healing rays into your energy field, you often need to begin to make space for the healing by clearing blocked, stuck, or stagnant energy that is already occupying your own or other people's energy fields. We will explore specific ways to do this in Chapter Seven as we begin to learn to use the Six-Step Spiritual Healing Protocol.

# CHAPTER SIX

# Working with Divine Knowing

ACCESSING DIVINE KNOWING MAY COME to some as fully developed capacities and to others only after years of inner seeking and work. My experience has been closer to the latter.

There was a time when I did not believe that it was possible to communicate with Divine Energy. Then after scores of workshops and books, I began to consider such communications might be possible. There was another stage where I desperately wanted to connect with Divine Wisdom, and still did not feel that I could make it happen. This was followed by years of extensive inner clearing and rebalancing around issues of anger and self-criticism to name a few. More years of deep conscious Silence occurred. Finally, there were the tiniest beginnings of a two-way conversation with Divine Knowing. After years of practice with various issues, concerns and many mistakes, I eventually was able to totally count on what I was receiving in Divine contact. This ability and blessing has changed my life so that I do not know how I would return to the state where I was not in constant contact with God/The Great Oneness/Yahweh.

## ACCESSING DIVINE KNOWING

At your core you are capable of Divine connection. You are an eternal being having a human experience. Therefore, within your own being is the capacity to access Divine Knowing. There are infinite ways to connect and you will develop your unique set of ways to connect, personally revealed during your seeking journey. The capacity to access Universal Knowing though only comes when you seek to have this intimate relationship with Divine Source.

The thought of having a personal relationship with God does not even appear until after you have been on a sacred seeking path for some time. *You first have to overcome numerous obstacles to even believe you are worthy or capable of having a personal relationship with All That Is/God/Divine Presence.*

When you are still in a state of duality, you are seeing yourself as completely separate from God. A personal, intimate relationship with Divine Presence in that mind space seems totally impossible. Then as you make peace with your self-judgments and criticisms, more of your loving self emerges from the rubble.

At one period in my life, I spent seven years in expanded Silence between five and eight hours a day, then taking up my normal life each day as well. This intentional Silence consisted of contemplative reading, journaling, clearing blocked energy, listening, and receiving spiritual training via Silence. I was guided to go within, to clear numerous problematic blocked energies I was experiencing. I filled many journals with all sorts of anger, rage, frustration, judgment, criticism, fear, guilt, and desire. I ranted on about my feelings concerning those in my life and was always brought back to what my part was in the imbalance. That was my personal spiritual training and this went on intensely for seven years. This process continues today and has expanded in scope to helping others learn to clear their blocked energies for themselves.

In my intense period of expanded Silence, I opened Sacred Space each day to do this work. Ways to open Sacred Space can be found in Chapter Seven in the Six-Step Spiritual Healing Protocol. In my mind, however, there was still a "me" space and a "God/Divine" space and they were separate. As I did this deep work, there would be times of intense vibrational experience when I simply had to stop all thought and be in that Divine connected energy. I had never experienced anything like that energy before in my life. I felt plugged into a huge vibrational energy force that encompassed me completely. Nothing else could be done but to sit and receive. It was a very clear signal to me to keep going, clearing, and looking at all places of imbalance within.

My first intense experiences with Divine Presence occurred when I was clearing all dross, anger, fear, and judgment that I knew about from my energy field. Seven years is an awful lot of blocked energy. At the end of seven years, this process shifted rather dramatically in that I was called to expand my work with clients and groups seeking Divine connection.

By the time you have personal experiences with Divine Presence, generally, you have been working with expanding spiritual awareness for some time, though not always. Continue to seek regardless of the outside circumstances or perhaps due to their persistent continuation in your life. Once you commit to a relationship with Divine Source, you are given all the help you need to bring about Peace and Balance. Keep returning to Sacred Space to continue clearing blocked energies and rebalancing, regardless of where you think you should be spiritually. Your perfect spiritual process is going to unfold as long as you remain committed to seeking.

As you begin to consider ways to access Universal or Divine Knowing, various methods will manifest before you. You often have to practice ways of being in contact with Divine Knowing so that you can really trust what you are receiving. *At your core, you are of Divine origination and substance. You are therefore wired for connection with the Greater Whole.* Setting your intention to personally connect and have an exchange with Divine Knowing Energy is an important first step.

I remember deeply wanting to be able to have visions of angels, cosmic light beings, meaningful colors, and facial recognition of the presence of Ascended Masters. I was constantly frustrated that these desired ways of connecting were not manifesting for me because I knew they were manifesting for others. I eventually had to clear that sense of insufficiency and failure regarding my desired way to connect with Spirit.

My beginning inklings of a connection with Spirit energy came as I realized I had a very clear knowing regarding optional choices, my path and direction. I began to know that one approach, book, or workshop was right for me and other options were not right for me. After years of this personal knowing, I slowly began to recognize that I would have a clear knowing that this person had cancer and that person was suffering from depression. I did not have visions though, almost never. I did not even recognize that what I had was direct Divine Knowing or connection to God Mind.

I continued for years, however, looking for my talents and abilities to manifest in particular ways. I continued to learn about a number of different ways to communicate with Divine Source. I could receive information with my non-dominant hand. This is a process of listening in Sacred Space with one's non-dominant hand, known as automatic writing. I would get very clear messages using my non-dominant hand because my mind was less active when using that hand, allowing clearer information to be received.

I also learned to use kinesiology as well as a pendulum to communicate with Divine Knowing. This is more thoroughly discussed in the next section.

As these ways of Divine communicating were manifesting though, I kept secretly wanting to be able to see, to be clairvoyant. I was shocked when one day a person said to me, "You are clairsentient and that is very rare". "Rare"! I did not even really have a good sense of what clairsentience was. Clairsentience is the ability to access knowledge for which there is no commonly recognized source or way to have obtained that knowledge. It comes from the Divine. It's another term for what I came to call Divine Knowing.

What a total delight this insight was for me. It was very freeing. I eventually began to honor the ways in which I could actually communicate with Divine Knowing. At that point, my talents and abilities took off in many directions. These events eventually enabled me to listen directly for Divine Insight and Guidance about all sorts of challenges and to get reliable guidance for self and others.

Divine Connection is waiting for you as soon as you clear the static energy in your mind and relationships that mainly consists of unfavorable views of self and others. You begin to recognize the presence of Divine Connection when you cultivate love, patience, tolerance, and forgiveness for yourself. When you clear all negative thoughts and feelings coming up about yourself and others, connection with Divine Source blossoms. This is an eternal process but beginning now means you will get closer and closer to manifesting this state of desired personal connection with Perfected Love/ Divine Source.

## KINESIOLOGY

My first introduction to working with Divine Knowing energy was through kinesiology. Kinesiology is the study of muscles and their movements especially as applied to physical conditioning. In his landmark book, *Power vs. Force*, David Hawkins relates a startling discovery by Dr. John Diamond.

> *… that indicator muscles would strengthen or weaken in the presences of positive or negative emotional and intellectual stimuli as well as physical stimuli. A smile will make you test strong, while the statement "I hate you" will make you test weak.*[6]

Why does kinesiology work? As we are Divine Beings, if we muscle-test others in specific ways, we can actually access Divine Knowing through their body and energy field. All bodies are of Divine origin and therefore speak to us clearly and accurately about all manner of issues. I spent a couple of years perfecting this method but I moved from there to use a pendulum in my working with Divine Knowing. I am partial to the pendulum now because I have more freedom to specifically frame the information I am interested in. If you are interested in learning a simple method of using kinesiology, read the Forward and Appendix B in David Hawkins' book, *Power vs. Force*[7].

I was introduced in Silence to the concept of working with Divine Preference. It is possible to ask between two options to see if there is Divine Preference for what is being asked. I found this easier to explore when with working with a pendulum.

By using kinesiology physically with another person, I could determine, for example, that a particular Yoga workshop was or was not compatible with that person. Their muscles would react strongly if the suggestion was compatible and would go limp if there was not a match. If I wanted to ask between two options though, I was stumped. Further, how could such information be determined with those who were not physically in my presence?

I found that using a pendulum in Sacred Space was every bit as accurate as physical kinesiology for long distance work as well as for those in my physical presence. While using a pendulum, I could frame my inquiry between two options and get a very clear answer as to whether there was a Divine Preference between the two options. This communications approach was additionally helpful, in that it did not require my touching other people, therefore enabling long distance healing. This method of human and Divine communications became preferable for me.

My introduction to using a pendulum in Sacred Space was given through Silence. I imagine there are practitioners who have training programs for using pendulums for skill development. Whatever the learning experience is, using the pendulum for Divine guidance requires that all work be done in Sacred Space.

One day a client came to me and asked if I could check out which of several locations was the best option for her to take a vacation. She had many different pros and cons for each location. Five locations were under consideration for her vacation. While in Sacred Space, the first step was to determine which individual locations were compatible with her energetically. That ruled out two locations, leaving three other locations under consideration.

I declared out loud that there was a Divine Preference between the remaining three locations for my client for her vacation. This was confirmed with the use of a pendulum. I repeated each location saying, "this location is the Divine Preference for (client name's) vacation". Two locations were indicated as not Divine Preference for my client. One was indicated as Divine Preference. I then shared this information with my client saying that this is only one way to determine compatibility and that her own instincts also needed to play a role in using this information.

I am sharing this process in a general way, though working in this form requires that all communications be stated in a declarative sentence to be agreed upon or not. Therefore, as noted, I did not ask questions, rather I stated potentially truthful sentences until one was confirmed.

There are numerous conditions required for clear and reliable two-way communications working with Divine Sources.

1. You need to be grounded to receive clear communications when working with Divine Source Energy. You can check this using kinesiology or a pendulum.
2. If you have a preference for a specific answer, you can energetically skew the seeking process. The ability to remain neutral when seeking Divine Knowing is essential.

3. Your chakras or energy wheels within your energetic field need to be open and balanced. You can check this using kinesiology or a pendulum.

4. You need to have completed your own work around a situation you are asking about; otherwise your personal unhealed issues can affect the answers you think you are receiving.

Imbalances in any of the above areas can detract from clear communications. I have also learned to open Sacred Space in all efforts when working with Divine Knowing. This insures that I am more likely to get reliable information. As there are all sorts of spirits in this dimension, we need to be sure by our command that we are in Sacred Space, and working with the Highest Light, however we define it.

Each new expansion of possible ways to communicate with Divine Source has been introduced to me in Silence. In the beginning, I was not even consciously seeking to inquire about Divine Preference. Even the thought that such communications was possible, was given. It would have never occurred to my human mind to seek Divine Preference information or insight. All my new learning has come as a result of being guided in Silence. As stated earlier, each person's journey is unique and unfolds in perfect timing. I share this information as one example of how your abilities to work with Spirit might develop.

## DIRECT KNOWING

As I began to truly appreciate and revel in the communication patterns that were evolving, other ways of hearing and communicating with Divine Presence showed up. I would know something to be true and eventually began to use the pendulum to check my intuition especially when working with others.

Eventually, in Sacred Space, words were given directly through me that were approximations in English of the nature of the healing and vibrations that were being received by clients. The process evolved and became one of listening and having the words come from my mouth without going through my mind. This is a synthesis of clairsentient and clairaudient talents. It is a strange experience in the beginning but as we use our talents and skills, they become second nature to us. This is sometimes referred to as direct God Knowing.

In my case, I had to work to acquire the facility to access Divine Knowing because much of my work now is teaching others to develop their own innate abilities through intention and practice. If I had simply manifested these abilities and talents with no effort on my part, I would have had no way to know how to help others develop mastery.

We all have intuition. The issue is discerning between when our human mind is speaking and when our Divine Knowing is informing us in the present moment. The discernment of this process can be greatly assisted, if so desired, through developing ways externally to check our accuracy.

One technique for working with Divine Knowing is to hold an item to your chest and let the body flow forwards or backwards as guided. You can test compatibility with any food substance, drink, or a medicine in this way. Hold an item to your chest, standing on both feet and let your body sway forwards or backwards with the intention of seeing if the item is compatible with you. When you sway forward the item is compatible with you. When you sway backwards, the item is not compatible with you. This is another way to check your intuition.

The ultimate goal is to have enough experience with your given methods of speaking with All That Is, that you can discern, and act on guidance with full confidence. This often takes practice or concerted effort to perfect. However, there are those among us whose discerning abilities have evolved organically as part of their overall spiritual evolution. Either way, as a result of seeking such Divine connection consciously or honoring the knowing we have been given, we can work with Divine Knowing and get reliable guidance for others and for ourselves.

As you honor and use the spiritual skills and talents you are being given, they expand, grow, and morph into other ways of connecting with Divine Knowing. As you hold the intention to receive and follow the Divine Guidance available to you, you will be met with all the options available for your mastery of a wide range of ways to access Divine Knowing.

## HEALING, HOMEOPATHY, AND STANDARD MEDICINE

My work is set in a both-and environment with regard to supporting all healing modalities that work for a person. There is a broad variety of healing approaches and modalities available to us. These can all be helpful at different times in our lives. Often, my clients seek my services when they have had chronic conditions or situations in their lives that are not healing with other medical or physiological help.

New clients will often ask me if they should stop seeing their oncologist, internist, gynecologist, eye doctor, homeopath, dentist, naturopath, psychologist, or general practitioner because they are working with me. My answer is, "not on my account". I am not a medical professional and I don't give medical advice. I see all kinds of healing including spiritual healing as an expanding continuum of available healing modalities. The issue is how to combine the various approaches and expertise for a successful healing approach for the client.

Spiritual healing is a joint process where I work from the client's knowing and interests to make suggestions for their healing and rebalancing that is indicated to me in Sacred Space. We are partners in their healing process. Without a client's commitment to inner healing, I can do very little to support them in spiritual healing.

Through spiritual insight and Divine Knowing, I have access to a broad range of information about specific energetic compatibilities for individuals regarding any area of their lives they are wondering about. This is because when working in Sacred Space, I am working in enhanced reality where all things are known and can be accessed.

I have access to a range of Divine Healing Energies that can be called in for a client for anything from a relationship to actual physical healing in the body itself. The scope of these healing options has expanded through the years. This is primarily so because I have been repeatedly reminded that my human mind thinks too narrowly about the breadth of Divine support and healing available to those of us in human body.

In my experience, all healing approaches manifest as both-and rather than either-or options. Even if all the blocked energies for a person manifesting depression are cleared in their energetic fields, their body still needs medical support until the chemistry in their bodies rebalances. Eventually as the body heals, clients get Divine guidance as to how and when to ease off medication.

The implementation of this information becomes a decision between my client and their doctor. Clients and I can check to see if a specific course of action is energetically compatible for the person. The client then takes all information and determines with their doctors how to proceed.

I had three clients, each with a different diagnosis; migraine headaches, insomnia, and asthma. Each client needed clearing for the same blocked energies of abuse and victim trauma energy. All three client's very different symptoms healed completely without ever focusing on the individual diagnoses themselves. Each client was carrying blocked abuse and victim trauma energies manifesting differently.

I find medical diagnoses useful in my work because they indicate the specific range of symptoms we are working with. Sometimes, however, we simply focus on the symptoms that need healing without ever having a medically derived diagnosis.

Those working with me have to make their own decisions as to how to integrate medical information with specific personal spiritual information. Often, clients with second and third-time cancer, continuing degradation of sight, or chronic imbalances, are more open and committed to spiritual healing because previous medical modalities have not brought about the desired healing in their bodies.

I augment what doctors are doing by supporting clients with inner clearing work that will enable them to heal mentally, physically, or emotionally. All blocked energy manifests in the body and in our lives as imbalance. Therefore, the process of working to clear this blocked energy is a foundational step to healing. Everything that is done spiritually to clear blocked energy enables bodies, minds, and emotions to heal.

In my utopian world, all medical doctors, mental health professionals, and spiritual healers would collaborate on approaches to healing, using their individual gifts and talents for the greatest good. Perhaps one day we will get there.

# CHAPTER SEVEN

# The Six-Step Spiritual Healing Protocol

ONE WAY TO ACCESS DIVINE HEALING is to call it forth into your energy fields and into this dimension. This Intelligence is always available to you but you must call it forth in ways you desire for healing. This can be done for individuals, situations, organizations, countries, and environmental issues, or for imbalances of any kind. The Six-Step Spiritual Healing Protocol can be used for anything where healing, rebalancing, and a call to wholeness is needed.

Divine Healing Intelligence is a form of Divine Knowing. I have been consciously working with this form of Divine Knowing for over 35 years. This healing protocol has been evolving for that full time as well. I was given bits of the full protocol along the way, as I was ready to use them and could understand them. This entire process of healing has been revealed to me while in Silence.

Last year, I began asking if the protocol was fully complete. That led to a number of refinements as well as other completely different approaches to healing being revealed. I continue to use all the following healing approaches with myself and in my spiritual healing practice. These healing approaches are being shared here for all those who are called to work in this way either for self-healing or for working with others. Perhaps what is shared here is fully complete but I tend to think that this is a snap shot in time for our use in the present moment that will continue to be simplified, refined, and expanded in years to come.

The most important prerequisite in the use of this healing protocol is to come to the use of it, knowing you are always heard and Spirit/All That Is will respond to you. What you or others think is being called forth and how you think it will manifest, requires that you remain non-attached to outcome. The loving intentions you use when calling forth healing for self or others is sufficient for you to trust that all that is needed is provided in the best possible ways, regardless of the outcome at the physical dimension. Authentic prayers for healing and wholeness are extraordinarily powerful. They are love in action and that is always powerful beyond your wildest imaginings.

When using the Six-Step Spiritual Healing Protocol, the italicized words are to be spoken out loud. Speaking these steps out loud gives form to the formless ideas and to the energies we are speaking about. This helps to activate these processes in our minds and in this physical world.

As you have free will, you must actually call forth the healing and rebalancing you are seeking. Your unfocused thoughts or vague prayers are not as effective as calling forth healing. This protocol produces desired results. Over the years, as more and more specificity has been added, the healings have become increasingly powerful and effective.

The experience of using a magnifying glass on a leaf comes to mind. When the sun's warmth is magnified through a magnifying glass and focused on a leaf, the heat begins to produce smoke and eventually fire that burns up the leaf. That leaf could sit all day in the sun and not burn up, in most environments. The focused nature of the sunlight produces this effect. The same is true of focusing prayers for healing.

The more specific the prayers are as to the specific areas of need, the more effective the Divine Healing Energy becomes when focused on these specific conditions and situations. For example, "Please help Jane feel better" is one level of prayer, and it will contribute to healing energy. "I call forth Divine Healing Energy for the rebalancing and strengthening of Jane's immune system and the clearing of all issues contributing to this compromised immune system" has more focus and specificity, therefore yielding a more targeted and thus powerful impact.

## GETTING STARTED

Here you will find a basic version of the Six-Step Spiritual Healing Protocol. It provides a view to the whole process in about two pages. In the following section of this chapter, I explain each of the six steps in more detail through answers to questions that clients frequently ask. I also suggest some alternatives and options for each step that may help you fit the protocol to your specific situation. Once you have a deeper understanding and experience with the protocol you may want to adjust some of the language to fit your inner knowing and faith tradition. Throughout the book I often use capitalized words and phrases to indicate the range of possible ways of speaking about spiritual knowing. If one way of phrasing these ideas is more comfortable for you than another, listen to that knowing and use it.

## THE SIX-STEP SPIRITUAL HEALING PROTOCOL

### 1. Open Sacred Space

*I open this Sacred Healing and Wisdom Circle and invite my I AM Energy to be present. I welcome the Angelic Host, the Ascended Masters, the Cosmic Light Beings of the Universe, the Devas and Nature Intelligences, and the Divine Healing Entities of the Highest Light from all traditions to partner with me in our shared knowing of the Oneness.*

### 2. Prepare and Listen

*I open my heart, mind, body, affairs, relationships and soul to Divine Presence to receive all that is available for me in this healing work today. I clear for the blocked energies of doubt and hesitation to call forth healing; for bias, preference, and attachment to specific desired outcomes; and for un-forgiveness of my self and others. I am listening and know ALL things are possible.*

### 3. Name the Imbalance

*My imbalance is [name of imbalance] trauma energy and all symptoms.*

EXAMPLES OF IMBALANCES: Guilt, abuse, pride, lying, unfaithfulness, fear of being out of Right Relationship with (person or situation), blame, resentment, death, fear, accident, loss, despondency, grief, shame, cancer, sciatic nerve imbalance, low back pain, insomnia, loneliness, judgment, impatience with self and life, apathy, addiction, abandonment, betrayal, rage, depression, etc.

### 4. Command Out and Clear Blocked Energies

*I call forth the Sacred Flame (or Divine Source, the Great I AM energy, My Divine Self, Eternal Flame, the Oneness the Christ energy) within me.*

*Sacred Flame, clear continuously all blocked emotional, mental, thermal, spiritual, hereditary line, karmic, curse, and spell energies back through all time and space from all lifetimes and originating sources, from all memories and patterns and down to the cells in my body manifesting as [name of imbalance] trauma energy and all symptoms.*

*Consume all blocked energies at the conscious, subconscious, unconscious, and supra-conscious levels contributing in any way to [name of imbalance] trauma energy and all symptoms.*

## 5. Maximize the Healing

*I call forth the appropriate Divine Healing Entities and the Angels to bring all needed Divine vibrational intervention healing at the physical level due to [name of imbalance] trauma energy and all symptoms at the highest possible rate of healing. I call forth Divine Stellar healing.*

*I am totally worthy of healing (or another affirmation).*

EXAMPLES OF AFFIRMATIONS: I am the Peace I seek. I am Perfect Love Energy. I am Light everlasting. I am Perfect Love in body. I am Capable and Loveable. Everything that is needed is provided. I am Eternal. I Am One with All That Is. I have all the chances I need to heal. I co-create with Divine Source. I respond to life in the present moment. I love myself (forgive myself, open to Divine Source, etc.) wholly and completely. I am the Healing Light I seek. I am patience (compassion, ease and grace, forgiveness, etc.) personified.

## 6. Close the Sacred Space

*With Divine partnership, we send these healing energies around the globe, to all those who can receive them this day.*

*I offer my deep appreciation to all Divine Beings carrying healing vibrations throughout this dimension to those who can receive them today. I give my profound thanks to the Sacred Healing and Wisdom Circle partners for their support and healing wisdom. I am so deeply blessed. My thanks. All this healing is manifesting in Divine Order. And So It is. Amen.*

© Robbins S. Hopkins 2017, Version 2.0

www.robbinshopkins.com

## 1. OPEN SACRED SPACE

*I open this Sacred Healing and Wisdom Circle and invite my I AM Energy to be present. I welcome the Angelic Host, the Ascended Masters, the Cosmic Light Beings of the Universe, the Devas and Nature Intelligences, and the Divine Healing Entities of the Highest Light from all traditions to partner with me in our shared knowing of the Oneness.*

### Why is it important to open sacred space first?

This healing protocol and all processes working with spiritual healing need to be conducted in Sacred Space. Without reservation, we are more effective working in partnership with Divine Beings of Highest Light in Sacred Space than working alone. When you ensure that you are working with Divine Beings of Highest Light everything happening in that space is in Right Relationship with All That Is/Divine Source/God.

There are all types of spirits along our airways. When individuals pass from human form, sometimes they do not leave this dimension but remain here in an energetic form. Most of us cannot see these beings. When you consciously work in Sacred Space, you know without a doubt that only the highest, most effective Divine Beings for your specific work will join with you to ensure the highest benevolent outcome manifests for the healing you are calling forth.

### What other ways can I use to open sacred space?

I have evolved two primary ways to open Sacred Space that come from my experiences of working with Divine Energy. The first way is included the basic Six-Step form above. Here is the second way:

*I open this Sacred Healing Space with my I AM Energy and call to join me all needed Divine Light Beings of highest light with a full myriad of gifts and abilities to work in partnership with me for healing.*

You can use these ways of opening Sacred Space until such time as you change it to wording that reflects your own experiences with Divine Energy.

## Do I need to open Sacred Space every time I call forth healing?

Yes, working in Sacred Space is essential to effective and responsible spiritual healing. If you find yourself working with people or individuals for an extended period of time, you can simply call for needed adjustments in the Sacred Healing and Wisdom Circle for each different focused time you wish to work in Sacred Space. If you have already opened Sacred Space, earlier in the day and you can say:

*I call for any changes required in Divine Beings needed for this new work with [name of person]. Thank you for all guidance, support and insight regarding this healing work.*

## What is the I AM Energy?

The I AM Energy as used here is our eternal energy that is always connected to The Great Oneness, that comprehensive Whole. You are constantly connected regardless of your outward knowing in a given lifetime. When you call this energy forth in Sacred Space, you activate deep knowing far beyond your conscious knowing. Some refer to this as intuitive knowing. Everyone has I AM Energy. However to activate it, you have to call it forth to be present within Sacred Space. I AM Energy is your eternal energy and can be understood as your eternal True Self, that which is always connected to the Greater Whole.

## What is the Angelic Host?

The Angelic Host encompasses the entire range of Angels including seraphim, cherubim, thrones, dominions, virtues, powers, principalities, angels, archangels and perhaps others not known to humans.

## Who are the Ascended Masters?

Ascended Masters are Beings from all traditions who have been in body and ascended to the Light after their passing. They have become consciously aware of their full eternal connection with God/All That Is/the Oneness while living in body.

## What are the Devas, Nature Spirits and Nature Intelligences?

Devas are Nature Spirits of all types including earth, air, water and fire elementals, sound and dance spirits, fauns and elves among many others. Nature Intelligences are various kinds of knowing energies residing within nature with vast influence on humans and all Earth Beings.

## What are Divine Healing Entities?

Divine Healing Entities of Highest Light are Light Beings committed to work with humans, animals, sea creatures, insects, birds, and all beings of the Earth from all Earth traditions. (See Chapter Eight for more information.)

## 2. PREPARE AND LISTEN

*I open my heart, mind, body, affairs, relationships and soul to Divine Presence to receive all that is available for me in this healing work today. I clear for the blocked energies of doubt and hesitation to call forth healing; for bias, preference, and attachment to specific desired outcomes; and for un-forgiveness of my self and others. I am listening and know ALL things are possible.*

## How do I prepare and listen?

Now that you have opened a sacred space, you need to open yourself and state this as an intention. Then you need to clear for blocked energies in your energy field that might interfere with hearing the guidance you seek.

## What other ways can I state my intention?

Here are three additional ways to state your intention to be open:

*I open my heart, mind, body, affairs, relationships, and soul to Divine Presence to receive all that is available for me in this healing work today.*

*I open all parts of me to Divine guidance, insight, wisdom, support, clarity, and suggestions as to how to proceed with this healing process.*

*I am listening to All That Is to hear how to proceed for maximum wisdom, healing support, and clearing intervention.*

## How do I listen?

Follow your chosen declaration of intent by sitting in the Sacred Space and truly listen. Whatever is on your mind will be known and responded to regarding the healing prayers you want to bring forth. At this point, you will most likely begin with a vague sense of what healing is needed. More specificity will be determined later in this process. The healing we call forth is always done with the goal being to return to Wholeness in all ways.

## What if I am blocked by doubt or uncertainty?

If you are you carrying doubt or hesitation energy about your ability to call forth healing and having it manifest, clear this uncertainty within your own being by saying:

*I command all blocked energies from emotional through spell energies and everything in between manifesting as healing uncertainty and hesitation trauma energy, and all symptoms to clear continuously from my conscious, subconscious, unconscious, and supra-conscious levels and come into Right Relationship with All That Is.*

## What if I am blocked by bias or preference?

If you are carrying a preference for a given outcome or for the form in which the healing is given, clear this preference energy from your energy field by saying:

*I command all blocked energies from emotional through spell energies and everything in between manifesting as outcome preference trauma energy and all symptoms, to clear continuously from my conscious, subconscious, unconscious, and supra-conscious levels and come into Right Relationship with All That Is.*

## What if I am blocked by un-forgiveness?

If you are carrying any un-forgiveness of self or others, clear this first by saying:

*I command all blocked energies from emotional through spell energies and everything in between manifesting as un-forgiveness trauma energy of myself/ name of person and all symptoms to clear from my conscious, subconscious, unconscious, and supra-conscious levels and come into Right Relationship with All That Is.*

## Should I write down what I hear?

As ideas come to you, you may find it helpful to take notes. You are listening so that you and the Divine Partners called forth can reach a shared knowing about the general focus of the healing that is needed. You are also determining if you have any clearing you need to undertake before moving forward.

## 3. NAME THE IMBALANCE

*My imbalance is [name of imbalance] trauma energy and all symptoms.*

Examples of imbalances: Guilt, abuse, pride, lying, unfaithfulness, fear of being out of Right Relationship with (person or situation), blame, resentment, death, fear, accident, loss, despondency, grief, shame, cancer, sciatic nerve imbalance, low back pain, insomnia, loneliness, judgment, impatience with self and life, apathy, addiction, abandonment, betrayal, rage, depression, etc.

## Why do you use the words "trauma energy?"

In Step 3, you are putting your general sense of the needed healing into specific language. The use of the words "trauma energy" has a specific meaning in this protocol. It refers to whole spectrum healing of the specific energy. Thus, if "guilt trauma energy" is the energy you are clearing, all guilt energy and all the ways it has affected you and others, and all symptoms of this is being named for healing. Here are some examples:

I am working with being lied to by [name of person]. I need to clear for my:

- mistrust trauma energy and all symptoms
- rage trauma energy and all symptoms
- judgment trauma energy and all symptoms

I am working with unfaithful spouse energy with [name of person]. I need to clear for my:

- anger and betrayal trauma energy and all symptoms
- abandonment trauma energy and all symptoms
- heartbreak trauma energy and all symptoms

I am having panic attacks. I need to clear for my:

- anxiety and tension trauma energy and all symptoms
- overwhelmed trauma energy and all symptoms
- fear of falling apart trauma energy and all symptoms
- shame trauma energy and all symptoms

You can call for your healing of mistrust energy with your mother (or name of person) as a focused healing topic. If, though you have been plagued by feeling mistrust with others throughout your life, you probably need a deeper clearing called forth. In this instance, "trauma energy" refers to whole spectrum of healing. This would be referred to as mistrust trauma energy and all symptoms. Trauma energy signifies a much more extensive set of energies being addressed than merely one instance of mistrust.

## Why do you clear for "all symptoms?"

The symptoms refer to all the reasons we have felt mistrust, all the behaviors we have exhibited as a result of that mistrust and all the impact we have caused with self and others by carrying mistrust energy in our field. We may know some of these consciously but there could be many other symptoms or manifestations we are not aware of which can be addressed by including all symptoms in our healing language.

## What is the key difference between steps 2 and 3 with regard to identifying the issues to work on?

In step 2 you are listening to determine what type of general imbalance you are focusing on. In step 3 you select the specific focus for your healing prayers and think about the specific feelings you have associated with that specific area, preparing for clearing those from your field.

## What does "being out of Right Relationship" mean?

Being out of Right Relationship with another refers to a Divine Order beyond the human scope of the imbalance. Using this term allows us to clear imbalances with others without completely knowing what is out of balance or why.

*Examples of possible imbalances (Also see Appendix.)*

- being out of Right Relationship with [person, place, thing] trauma energy and all symptoms
- fear of failure (or embarrassment, loss of status, making the wrong decision, moving forward, getting hurt, missing out, etc.) trauma energy and all symptoms
- guilt (or shame, desire, pride, apathy, rage, blame, attack, resentment, anger, anxiety, ego, impatience) trauma energy and all symptoms
- child (or sexual, verbal, mental, physical, emotional) abuse trauma energy and all symptoms
- marriage (or lying, divorce, birth, unfaithfulness, immigration, death, accident) trauma energy and all symptoms
- loss of spouse (or child, parent, pet, home, job, brother, sister, girl/boyfriend, health) trauma energy and all symptoms
- memory (or digestive, foot, knee, hip, hearing, vision, kidney, shoulder, breathing, weight, acne, sciatic nerve, low back pain) imbalance trauma energy and all symptoms
- blood (or bone, brain, lung, breast, uterine) cancer trauma energy and all symptoms
- self-deprecation (or insomnia, impatience with self and life, panic attack, un-worthiness, frustration with self) trauma energy and all symptoms
- fear for [person, place or thing] trauma energy and all symptoms
- worry (or depression, un-forgiveness, punishment, negative thinking, mistrust, perfection, unhappiness, pushing, loneliness) trauma energy and all symptoms
- addiction to alcohol (or spending, cigarettes, gambling, pornography, food) trauma energy and all symptoms

- feeling unsafe (or sad, lost, afraid, betrayed, worried, ungrateful, cheated, badly treated, punished, ignored) trauma energy and all symptoms
- abandonment (or betrayal, violence, unworthiness, surgical, procreation, judgment, illness, jealousy) trauma energy and all symptom
- Parkinson's Disease (or ALS, HIV-AIDS, Alzheimer's, Clymidea, Herpes) trauma energy and all symptoms

## 4. COMMAND OUT AND CLEAR BLOCKED ENERGIES

*I call forth the Sacred Flame (or Divine Source, the Great I AM energy, My Divine Self, Eternal Flame, the Oneness the Christ energy) within me.*

*Sacred Flame, clear continuously all blocked emotional, mental, thermal, spiritual, hereditary line, karmic, curse, and spell energies back through all time and space from all lifetimes and originating sources, from all memories and patterns and down to the cells in my body manifesting as [name of imbalance] trauma energy and all symptoms.*

*Consume all blocked energies at the conscious, subconscious, unconscious, and supra-conscious levels contributing in any way to [name of imbalance] trauma energy and all symptoms.*

### Why do you use the phrase "Sacred Flame"?

The Sacred Flame is one image of the presence of Source Energy within all of us. You could also use Divine Spirit within, the Christ within, My Divine Self, my Eternal Oneness, the Eternal Flame, the Violet Flame, Perfect Love, etc., as you are guided. In this protocol, we work with the Sacred Flame, the Violet Flame or the Eternal Flame, all of which are terms used to indicate the Divine Spark within all sentient beings.

The Ascended Master, Saint Germain is known among other things as the master teacher of the Violet Flame. Writings ascribed to Saint Germain in his I AM series of books thoroughly explore working with the Violet Flame in many situations.[8] We use the Violet, Eternal or Sacred Flame as terms to describe the Divine Spark within each person that with focused intention, we can use for healing.

## Why do you name all the different kinds of energies needed for clearing?

All the different types of energies needing clearing are named so that wherever the blocked energy may reside it will be directly addressed. This is the most comprehensive way to get to all blocked energy.

The emotional body is the closest energy field to the physical body. You feel issues in your emotional body very strongly and they can manifest in countless ways in the body. Anger, blame, guilt, shame, apathy, pride, anxiety, jealousy, and all other emotions except fear reside in the emotional body. Fear resides in the spiritual body. For example, if there is anger in the emotional body with regard to an intimate, this may manifest as a urinary tract infection. If there is resentment towards a parent, this can manifest as imbalances in the knees.

The mental body is the second energetic field from the physical body. For example, if you *think* you are unprepared for your job, this can manifest as ineffective behaviors on the job. Until the blocking mental thought is cleared, mistakes and conflict can manifest on the job. This is the "knowing body's" way of signaling there is imbalance.

The thermal body is the third energy field from the physical body. The thermal body is where all self-protective energies reside. If you have blocked energies there, they can manifest as being unable to emotionally bond with others or possibly as being unable to take any risks with money or employment due to blocked self-protective energy.

The spiritual body is the fourth energetic field from the physical body. Blocked energies in the spiritual field are fear and doubt. If you carry doubt about your self-worth in your spiritual body, you could manifest a string of bad relationships or the inability to progress in your work setting. If you carry fear for your job, you could manifest anger and competitive behaviors whenever you feel threatened at work.

One important principle to remember is if you have blocked emotional energy in your energetic field, which is closest to the physical body, you also have blocks in all the other energetic fields connected with the body as well. In other words, if there is blocked emotional energy, you also have blocked mental, thermal and spiritual blocked energies as well.

## What is hereditary line energy?

Hereditary line energy is the result of energy patterns being passed from our father or mother's line over generations. This energy is often present in the household you grew up in. This is not gene-induced energy. This pertains to energetic patterning. Perhaps your father was exceedingly generous to a fault towards all who asked and you have that same tendency in your life as well. You can't say no, ever, regardless of whether the request is compatible with you or not. If this blocked energy is cleared, the manifestation of these behaviors in your life will shift.

## What are karmic, curse, and spell energies?

Karmic energy is energy you carry as a result of unhealed energies in previous states, lifetimes, or earlier in your present lifetime. This energy is most often thought of as a debt energy that you need to make amends for in the present lifetime. This can manifest, for example, as a contentious relationship without any seeming explanation in this lifetime. This can also manifest as being unable to keep good employees due to unfair employee practices earlier in the company's history.

Curse energy is an energy I think of as not "really" existing. You may still carry the power of a curse once voiced but you have given your own power to the stated curse. The curse itself carries no power other than what you give it. For example, you may have grown up being repeatedly told you are not going to amount to anything in this lifetime. Especially when curse energy is felt before you are seven, it can remain in your unconscious energy field. You can manifest years of failures before you realize that you carry such curse energy.

Spell energy refers to energy that has a beginning and an end. This energy may no longer be present in your conscious present life but the energy remains in your energetic field. Perhaps you are afraid of the dark at age 35. This fear could be lodged in your energy field due to scary experiences you had years ago, when away at camp, for example. Though the experiences have stopped, the spell energy is present in your unconscious field and does affect you. This also refers to blocked energies you may have brought with you from a previous incarnation.

As it is often unclear which of these energies are affecting you, it is the most efficient to clear for all of them when doing this work. If you are repeating blocked energy clearings with regard to different individuals or different circumstances following upon each other, you can shorten this to *clear all blocked emotional through spell energies and everything in between manifesting as [name of imbalance], for example, mistrust.*

## Why is it important to clear blocked energy in the different levels of consciousness?

You can call for the emotional through spell energies to be cleared and they will clear from the conscious level. However, if some of these same energies are also found at other levels of consciousness, the manifestations or symptoms being addressed cannot completely rebalance.

The conscious level of awareness is that which a person knows. People often know why they are angry. Sometimes though, you are angry and do not know exactly why you feel this way. This can be because the blocked energy fueling the anger is not in your conscious field. Somehow the anger has slipped out but you do not know exactly where the anger came from. The blocked energy can reside in the subconscious field, which is your thinking field. You can have the thought that you have been mistreated and that can fuel your anger without your being consciously aware of how this is happening.

The blocked energy can also be in your unconscious field that may have been experienced before your were conscious. Children generally become conscious around seven years of age. If you have been abused when you were a young child but do not actually recall this, you may still have feelings of mistrust and vulnerability without understanding why those feelings exist.

The blocked energies can also be in the supra-conscious field (at the soul level) and have been with you for lifetimes. Unhealed energy can be with you for years and lifetimes before you begin to heal it at all levels of your being.

Supra-conscious blocked energy is soul energy. You can carry unhealed energy from your soul level from previous lifetimes or experiences. Frequently chronic imbalances have blocked energies in the unconscious and supra-conscious level. So, for example, chronic insomnia or chronic depression is often due to unhealed energies in the unconscious and supra-conscious levels.

In many ways, you are run by your unknown energies. If you have guilt feelings you are aware of, it is likely you have lots more guilt hidden from you in your other levels of consciousness. I have asked hundreds of individuals if they feel, anger, fear, guilt, or judgment, etc. regarding a certain person, and they will say, "no, not at all". Energetically then, I will often find this energy at other levels of consciousness. In many cases this helps explain why undesirable strong feelings and subsequent actions manifest without any seemingly logical reason.

Until all blocked emotional, mental, thermal, spiritual, hereditary line, karmic, curse and spell energies at the conscious, subconscious, unconscious, and supra-conscious levels are cleared with respect to a particular trauma energy, you are unable to fully and permanently heal.

## Why do I need to clear blocked energy from memories and patterns in my energetic field through all time and space?

Blocked energies can reside in your memories and patterns found in your energetic fields from any form or formless state you have ever been in. Therefore these blocked energies can cause imbalances at the physical level. Blocked memories and patterns are extremely difficult to observe as they are often enmeshed in thoughts and actions of our daily lives. As these energies are very hard to pinpoint, we use this language to pinpoint the entire type of energy that needs clearing. If you want full healing of all blocked energy, you need to include these types of energies in every call for healing.

## Are there differences in clearing blocked energies for physical rather than mental or emotional imbalances?

All imbalances manifesting in your mind, body, relationships, affairs, lives and souls are due to blocked energy found somewhere in your energy field or your eternal soul. Thankfully though, the process for clearing imbalances of any kind is the same.

Viruses are contracted or not, often depending on the strength of your immune system. Two people can be exposed to the same virus and one contracts the virus and the other person does not. You have to look behind the presenting imbalance, the virus, for all blocked energy that may be affecting the body, and thereby the immune system, that is speaking to you as a virus. So, if you have a virus, blocked energy from a relationship, job, sleep or diet, for example, may need to be cleared to enable the immune system to heal. When the immune system comes into balance, the virus can fully heal as well. You have to scan your life, in Sacred Space, and make a guess about what could be affecting your immune system. Begin the healing there.

When you are depressed, clearing all blocked energy that is showing up as depression, enables complete healing of depression and related symptoms. This is true for all imbalances manifesting in our energetic fields, emotional, mental, spiritual and physical bodies. All blocked or undesirable energies in our field will dissipate if we deny them a place to stay. Command them out!

## How do I incorporate "color ray energy"

You can call forth Divine color ray energy to replace the dense blocked energies in the energy field and physical body. Divine color ray energy is of very high vibration and supports energetic and physical changes in the body and energy field.

You can say: *I call forth the Divine color ray of green for forgiveness into my energy field and physical body for all available rebalancing and healing.* (See Chapter Five, Light Vibrations, color ray chart.)

## How can I make Step 4 more specific to my situation?

One way to make Step 4 more specific to your situation is to add a specific name to the opening phrase. You can say: *I call forth the Eternal Flame within me (or name of person, organization, group, etc.)*

For all healing, the more specific you are in the naming the focus of the energy being called forth including how you see it manifesting, the more effective the healing is.

In other words, when you say: "Please help Martha heal from migraines", this is less effective than this Six-Step Spiritual Healing Protocol. In the example above, there is a presumption that you are speaking to an Entity outside of Martha for her healing. This is energetically inaccurate throughout the Universe and thus weakens the call for healing. In the Six-Step Spiritual Healing Protocol, we begin with the healing being called from the Sacred Flame within ourselves or within the individual involved.

Divine Presence is within all of us. Therefore, calling for healing is more effective when consistent with the reality of Universal Energy. When we call for the Sacred Flame within Martha to clear blocked energies, Martha's knowing body will then be able to heal itself. She may also need specific Divine help, medicine, or physical treatments to support her body in healing but she will be able to heal because the root issues often unseen and unknown to her, causing the imbalance, have been cleared.

## How do I use all the types of needed clearing for a single imbalance?

These following examples all need to be used consecutively with a single imbalance for maximum healing.

*Sacred Violet Flame come forth from within me and clear continuously the blocked emotional, mental, thermal, spiritual, hereditary line, karmic, curse, and spell energies manifesting as [name of imbalance, e.g. depression] trauma energy and all symptoms.*

*Clear all blocked energies from original sources, back through all time and space, down to the cells in the body, from memories and patterns in the energetic field from the conscious, subconscious, unconscious, and supra-conscious levels manifesting as depression (or anger at daily life, being out of Right Relationship with myself, divorce, depression, anxiety, failure to thrive physically, financially, professionally, fear of going outside, obesity, self-hatred, self-judgment, shame, apathy, migraine, digestion, concussion, relationship) trauma energy and all symptoms.*

*I call forth the appropriate Divine Healing Entities and Angels for Divine vibrational healing intervention with all physical symptoms from depression (or epileptic seizures, job loss, parent's death, anxiety, addiction, judgment, hearing loss, insomnia) until such time as all symptoms come into Right Relationship with All That Is.*

*Divine Presence; replace the dense, heavy blocked energy spaces within me [name the person] with the Divine violet color ray for balance and Divine perfection. (See Chapter Five, Light Vibrations, color ray chart)*

## Do I need to call for each type of clearing at this level separately or can I combine them?

As you gain more experience and inner knowing you can combine types of clearing for maximum effect in healing. Always make sure to include Divine vibrational healing when support is needed for the body at the physical level. Frequently, both unseen blocked energies need to clear and specific physical healing needs to be called in for complete healing. Here are some examples combining the various types of clearing in Step 4.

*Sacred Flame within me, come forth. Clear continuously all emotional, mental, thermal, spiritual, hereditary line, karmic, curse and spell energies manifesting as [name of imbalance, e.g. insomnia] trauma energy and all symptoms.*

*Come forth Eternal Violet Flame within me (or name of person, town, office, company, etc.) Clear continuously all blocked energies from emotional to spell energies and everything in between contributing to [name of imbalance, e.g. dishonesty] trauma energy and all symptoms.*

*Sacred Flame within me, clear blocked energies from all memories and patterns in the energetic field, down to the cells in the body, back through all time and space and from originating sources manifesting as [name of imbalance, e.g. jealousy] trauma energy and all symptoms.*

*Sacred flame within me (or name the person, organization, group, etc.) clear continuously all blocked emotional through spell energies and everything in between from the conscious, subconscious, unconscious, and supra-conscious levels, from all memories and patterns in the energetic field, back through all time and space, down to the cells in my body (or bodies of all employees, bodies of all team members, etc.) manifesting as [name of imbalance] trauma energy and all symptoms.*

*I call the appropriate Divine Healing Entities and the Angels to come forth with all needed Divine vibrational healing for my [name of person] left kidney [name the body part] until such time as it comes into balance with Divine Source.*

*I call forth the appropriate Himalayan Healing Entities and the Angels working with the [name the body part] to bring Divine healing vibrations to me [name of person] for all forms of cancer in my/his/her [name the body part] until such time as the [name the body part] is in balance with All That Is. (See Chapter Eight, Healing Entity Groups for further specifics).*

*I call forth the Divine pink color ray for Unconditional Love to fill all dense spaces in my body (or name person, situation, or organization) and my/her/ its energy field. (See Chapter Five, Light Vibrations for Divine color chart.).*

## 5. MAXIMIZE THE HEALING

*I call forth the appropriate Divine Healing Entities and the Angels to bring all needed Divine vibrational intervention healing at the physical level due to [name of imbalance] trauma energy and all symptoms at the highest possible rate of healing. I call forth Divine Stellar healing.*

*I am totally worthy of healing (or another affirmation).*

EXAMPLES OF AFFIRMATIONS: I am the Peace I seek. I am Perfect Love Energy. I am Light everlasting. I am Perfect Love in body. I am Capable and Loveable. Everything that is needed is provided. I am Eternal. I Am One with All That Is. I have all the chances I need to heal. I co-create with Divine Source. I respond to life in the present moment. I <u>love myself</u> (forgive myself, open to Divine Source, etc.) wholly and completely. I am the Healing Light I seek. I am <u>patience</u> (compassion, ease and grace, forgiveness, etc.) personified.

## How is this step different from calling forth blocked energy in step 4?

When all blocked unseen energy is cleared regarding a specific trauma energy, as a result of step 4, there are often physical symptoms still needing healing. Both unseen energies and the energy of the body need attention for full healing. This physical healing can come from Divine Beings, Divine Stellar Energies as well as from homeopathic preparations, supplements, herbs, and prescription drugs. All these types of healing energies and substances can support healing at the physical level. For example, you can be free from the blocked energies manifesting as digestive tract trauma energy and still need Divine vibrational healing at the physical level for the stomach and colon.

## What is Divine vibrational intervention healing

Divine vibrational intervention healing is healing that can be called from Divine Healing Entities working in partnership with us in Sacred Space. This healing energy can also be called from the Angelic Host, Ascended Masters of all traditions, Cosmic Light Being of the Universe, Devas and Nature Intelligences to name a few sources. Each of these types of Divine Beings and Intelligences can aid us in healing. They do this by raising our vibrations to a level that eventually comes into Right Relationship with

All That Is/The Great Spirit and manifests as body healing. (See Chapter Eight, on Healing Entity Groups.)

It is important to be as specific as possible regarding what area of the body needs to be addressed with Divine vibrational intervention healing. It is most fully covered by including a call for continuous healing until the body part or system comes into Right Relationship with All That Is or Divine Oneness. I learned while in meditative Silence to call for the combination of Divine Healing Entities and Angels working together as the best combination for healing the body with Divine vibrational intervention healing.

You can add additional specificity by saying: *I call forth the most appropriate Divine Healing Entities and Angels available for Divine vibrational intervention healing for my (or name of person) [left eye, right hip, pancreas, right lung, GI tract, blocked cardiac artery, etc.] on a continuous basis until such time as the [specific body part] is in Right Relationship with All That Is.*

## How do I call forth an increased rate of healing?

We are Divine Beings having a human experience. Therefore, we have the authority to call forth all aspects of healing we desire. We can call for an increased rate of healing to speed up the healing process itself. If you have the gift of clairaudience or can use a pendulum, listen for the specific rate of accelerated healing that is optimal for you or for the person being supported. Alternatively, call for the highest healing rate possible for this situation or person. All that is possible will manifest.

Here are some examples:

*I call forth a 10-fold increase in the normal healing rate for all blocked energies manifesting as contentious energy with my spouse (or broken left rib, eye, alcohol misuse, loss, fear, shame, mistrust of my sister) trauma energy and all the ways this is showing up in my life.*

*I call forth the highest possible increased rate of healing for financial management (or forgiveness of myself, my cancerous cells, my lethargy, my viral infection, my envy of my brother, gambling) trauma energy and all symptoms.*

## What is Divine Stellar Healing?

Divine Stellar healing energy is the energy of the sun, moon, and stars. Each of these celestial bodies is made from the exact chemical compounds, as are we, however, manifesting in different forms.

As Carl Sagan famously explained in Cosmos,

*The nitrogen in our DNA, the calcium in our teeth, the iron in our blood, the carbon in our apple pies were made in the interiors of collapsing stars. We are made of starstuff.*[9]

Therefore healing energies from these sources are readily available to our bodies and easily received as support and healing energy for our bodies. The healing energies from these celestial bodies are compatible with our bodies. Further, they go beyond the resources of allopathic and homeopathic medicine, and alternative healing modalities while remaining completely compatible with these healing approaches as well.

## Why are affirmations important?

Affirmations are a powerful way to replace old habits with higher vibrational, powerful truths through declaration. Suppose you are being plagued by fears of being destitute. That old habit of feeling the fear and helplessness around issues of abundance can be replaced by affirming higher vibrational truths that "override" the old humanly created tapes in your head. For example, you could affirm any of the following:

- All that is needed is provided
- I am deserving of prosperity and abundance
- Abundance and prosperity are manifesting as I face my old fears of lack and supply.

To come up with appropriate and useful affirmations, you need to practice writing them and saying the affirmations in a number of ways. Then, choose the ones that feel the most powerful to you and repeat them out loud, often. As stated earlier, when we speak out loud, we give form and substance to the concepts and therefore power to what we are calling forth in this dimension.

Affirmations serve to retrain the mind to the realities of Divine Truth. The mind is greatly influenced by all sorts of human conditioning, collective consciousness, old experiences and messages in the subconscious or unconscious body. If you truly want to affirm the power and presence of Divine Oneness/God/All That Is, you have to retrain your mind in ways you want it to think. Use some of the examples below or create your own affirmations.

Examples of affirmations:

- I am the Peace I seek.
- I am Perfect Love Energy.
- I am Light everlasting
- I am Perfect Love in body.
- I am Capable and Loveable.
- Everything that is needed is provided.
- I am Eternal.
- I Am One with All That Is.
- I co-create with Divine Source.
- I respond to life in the present moment.
- I love (or forgive, trust, am patient with, at Peace with) myself wholly and completely.
- I am the Healing Light I seek.
- I am Patience (or Love, Grace, Hope, Kindness) personified.
- My intentions to partner with The Divine manifest in perfect ways.
- My body manifests the healing energy I seek.
- My needs are fully met in abundance.
- My forgiving self is expanding.

## 6. CLOSE THE SACRED SPACE

*With Divine partnership, we send these healing energies around the globe, to all those who can receive them this day.*

*I offer my deep appreciation to all Divine Beings carrying healing vibrations throughout this dimension to those who can receive them today. I give my profound thanks to the Sacred Healing and Wisdom Circle partners for their support and healing wisdom. I am so deeply blessed. My thanks. All this healing is manifesting in Divine Order. And So It is. Amen.*

### Why do we send these healings around the globe?

When healing vibrations have been received in this dimension, due to your calling them forth, they can be received by anyone, anywhere in this dimension who is seeking or needing such help. The "we" in the above example refers to you and all the Divine Beings working with you who can literally bring these healing vibrations to others. We increase our healing impact by sending the received blessings out to all others around the globe needing similar healing.

Here are some alternative ways of sending the healing around the globe:

*We send out all the healing energy and blessings received here today to thousands or millions of others around the globe who need this healing energy and support today.*

*We send all healing vibrations received here today across this planet to all those who need this type of healing today.*

*Why do we thank the Divine Beings and our partners in the Sacred Healing and Wisdom Circle?*

It is always enriching to strengthen your partnership with Divine Beings. Therefore, it is a powerful step to offer thanks to those working with you. The acknowledgement of the human and Divine partnership you work within always enhances your ability to work together more effectively. It is in Right Relationship to offer appreciation to Divine Entities, Ascended Master, Angels, Nature Intelligences, and others who work with you and who carry these healing vibrations to others around the globe. You can in this way call in healing for all those in need.

Think about how you want to give thanks for the Spiritual Partnership that has been formed to support you. How do you want to show gratitude for the healing energy that has manifest as a result of this Sacred Healing Circle? However you give thanks will be wholly sufficient.

Here are some examples:

*I am deeply grateful to all the Divine Beings working with me today and for carrying healing vibrations throughout this dimension to those in need.*

*My profound thanks to all Divine Entities in this Sacred Healing and Wisdom Circle for supporting me and for offering healing energy to millions of others in need, across the globe.*

*I am deeply grateful for the love and healing support of the Divine Beings gathered here to support me in this Sacred Healing and Wisdom circle. I feel very blessed.*

*I am deeply grateful for the insight, guidance and healing grace given today in partnership with Divine Entities partnering with me in this Sacred Healing and Wisdom Circle.*

## PHYSICAL IMPACTS OF SPIRITUAL HEALING

As with healing of any kind, there is detoxification following spiritual healing. When the vibrations in our bodies are raised through the clearing of blocked energy, the body sloughs off toxins in response, as part of the healing process. This often results in feelings of lethargy; fatigue, low energy, or bowel imbalances. It can even involve vomiting when one is working with cancer. There can be other less frequently seen detox symptoms that manifest as thirst, inability to sleep, nightmares, rashes, dizziness, sweats, and the need to sleep long hours.

Detox can show up in an infinite numbers of ways so anything out of the ordinary the day after healing, is most probably detox. If these manifestations occur, drink extra amounts of water or herbal tea to aid in the clearing of toxins and rest whenever possible until the detox symptoms pass. Eating lightly will help the body have the reserves it needs for healing rather than using the reduced available energy for digesting heavy, sweet, or fried foods. You need to act as if major healing has occurred because it most certainly has occurred.

The day after spiritual healing and clearing of blocked energy is usually the most severe day for detoxification. In many cases, those going through this for the first time can often feel that nothing has happened after the spiritual healing because the symptoms felt in detox are often similar to the symptoms being addressed by the healing. There is often a period after the spiritual healing has been called in and before the healing is fully manifest in the physical body. It is an in-between time.

As mentioned earlier, the last place the healing manifests is in the physical body because it is much denser than the energy in the emotional, mental, thermal or spiritual bodies. Each person differs regarding the severity of detox symptoms. I have known people to not be able to get out of bed the day after healing, including myself. Generally, as the days continue, the detox symptoms lessen in intensity. However, the symptoms can last two to five days on average or more.

The detox experience occurs for most people whenever spiritual healing is received at the conscious level. However, there is usually little or no detox if the healing is addressing the subconscious, unconscious or supra-conscious levels of the energetic field. These fields do not exist within the physical body and therefore do not affect the physical body with detox.

With regard to Divine vibrational healing interventions in the body, there will often be restrictions indicated such as no lifting for 14 days or no exercise for two days after some Divine vibrational healing interventions. If you are not able to discern this, to be on the safe side, any time you are working with muscles, arteries or veins, restrict lifting for 14 days and hard aerobic workouts for 10 days. Walking is often fine two days after the healing but tiredness indicates that care needs to be taken. There may also be tiredness or other symptoms of detox experienced with this type of spiritual healing.

The general stance to take with all spiritual healing is that it has been called for, received and your body is busily trying to adjust to the clearings and healing that have taken place. A new balanced period will follow but detox is a natural occurrence of spiritual healing.

# CHAPTER EIGHT

# Expanded Protocol Topics

YOU CAN ALWAYS GO DEEPER. In the previous chapter, I introduced you to the Six-Step Spiritual Healing Protocol. The protocol is the framework on which you can array your deeper understanding and experience as you develop your confidence and knowing. This chapter and the following chapters explain in more detail, key aspects of the protocol that I have touched on in the questions and answers sections in Chapter Seven. In Chapter Twelve, there is step-by-step summary of healing approaches you can use to put all of these techniques together.

## UNCONSCIOUS AND SUPRA-CONSCIOUS TRAUMA ENERGY

When you begin spiritual healing, you naturally begin with imbalances and issues that are consciously known to you. You know when you feel angry, vengeful, unforgiving, lost, afraid or envious. You can feel these feelings inside yourself, affecting how you interact with others, how you feel about yourself, and how you make sense out of the world. There can be years and years of clearing blocked or unhelpful energies and emotions you are aware of before you come to a place where there are still imbalances in your energy field or body that are not healing.

Sometime in the early stages of spiritual healing, you begin to also become aware of thoughts about yourself and others that are not helpful and out of balance. You begin to be aware of judgments, negative characterizations, and expectations or thought patterns that govern your thoughts about yourself and others. These can be greatly affected by how you grow up, where you grow up and what you are taught about right and wrong, good and bad, acceptable and unacceptable. When you begin to work on healing your thoughts, you move into work with subconscious energy. This is where many people remain for lifetimes often working with what is known about thoughts and feelings and addressing those imbalances. This work is crucial to leading you deeper and deeper into how you feel separated and set apart from Divine Source/God/All That Is. All spiritual work begins with the examination of your feeling and thoughts.

You have to begin with what you know is out of balance and work there for healing and release. There comes a time though when you may have worked on issues over and over again and they keep showing up in your life experiences and feelings. Take for example, guilt. You may have cleared and cleared for guilt energies for years and find that guilt is still in your energy field. You may not even be able to put your finger on the type of guilt you feel but that imprint is still in your field. When this begins to happen, it can be a sign that the blocked energies that are affecting you originate in the unconscious or supra-conscious parts of your being.

Unconscious energy is energy that is completely unknown to you. Supra-conscious energy is soul energy that has been with you through many forms or out of form. You can compare conscious and unconscious energy to an iceberg. You can see a small part of an iceberg above water's edge that would be comparable to conscious energy. However, the vast remainder of the iceberg is under the water, unknown and unseen by you. Most of the iceberg in fact is hidden deep in the water. This is a good metaphor for unconscious energy.

Unconscious energy is energy you are not aware of at all. You can become aware of it if you manifest some thought or emotion over and over again that you have worked to release from your conscious field and it is still showing up in your energy field. When actions or perceptions, feelings or thoughts keep coming up for seemingly no reason, there is a real chance the source is the unconscious or supra-conscious energy. There are energies in your energy field about which you are completely unaware. All human beings are more than our bodies. We each have energy fields surrounding us. Unconscious and supra-conscious energy have a direct impact on physical and interactive patterns in our bodies and relationships.

Supra-conscious energy is soul energy that can be equally challenging to identify as it has been traveling with you through your eternal existence. Therefore, these energies or levels of consciousness usually make themselves known through chronic illnesses and imbalances that cannot be attributed to conscious or subconscious energy. I think of supra-conscious energy as unconscious energy that is even more deeply buried from conscious knowing. Why are you afraid of heights or of looking over the edge of a canyon or afraid of being attacked at night, afraid of bees or afraid of being destitute, especially when nothing in your known past can explain these reactions to life? Some of these manifestations could be blocked supra-conscious energy that has traveled with you for lifetimes of existence in form or out of form. You have no conscious access to supra-conscious energy, so you are likely to identify this blocked energy as being due to chronic patterns of illness or imbalance. This would be only a partial assessment.

Imbalance issues throughout your whole body may be another indication. The general tendency is to look at each imbalance separately. One client I worked with was manifesting imbalances with his wrist, hearing, prostate gland, energy levels and memory. I was led to look at the unconscious and supra-conscious level energies that might be producing all these imbalances. I was guided to clear for unconscious and supra-conscious guilt and judgment trauma energy and all symptoms including all of the ways this was showing up in his body. Though everything did not work perfectly at the end of that day, there was no further specific work indicated for the specific imbalances. I understood this to mean that the core sources of these physical imbalances were unconscious and supra-conscious blocked energies. Energetically that clearing for the unconscious and supra-conscious guilt and judgment trauma energy was huge for him.

*A Course in Miracles,* [10] states that guilt trauma energy causes all suffering. Imagine if that guilt resides in your unconscious. It keeps showing up over and over again because you are not aware of what the body is trying to tell you. Clearing for those carrying unconscious guilt trauma has been profound when this energy has left specific energy fields.

In the *Disappearance of the Universe,* Gary Renard[11]also points to unconscious guilt as the main cause of suffering. When we initially separate from the Oneness to come into body, we naturally have great guilt that we have left that loving space to have a seemingly independent human experience. This is true for almost all those in body, except for those who have already ascended and have consciously returned to serve humans in this dimension.

When unconscious or soul patterns exist, they essentially program our thinking and our minds. We have almost no way to identify these issues unless we are on a seeking path and happen to come across information on clearing unconscious or supra-conscious energy.

Entire nations, governments, families, organizations, schools, wars, criminal activities, and military units take their form from the programming of unconscious energy. Virtually all shame, guilt, apathy, grief, fear, anger, desire, pride, judgment, and un-forgiveness stem from the unconscious parts of our brains. You may see an indication of these imbalances in your life interactions but when they are repeated over years and circumstances, they most probably reside in our unconscious mind.

From Divine Knowing, it has been indicated that as much as 99% of our mental programming can be directed by our unconscious mind. Therefore, all sorts of fears, beliefs, reactions and interactions we do not know about or understand can be affecting your physical body and our entire world. We seemingly have no way of effectively addressing such imbalances, as we do not know about their sources.

When you have sought to clear a number of imbalances that you are aware of and you still notice imbalances in your being that you can't seem to affect, you need to consider clearing specific unconscious and supra-conscious trauma energy and all symptoms. (See Six-Step Spiritual Healing Protocol for more specifics.)

The best way to identify potential sources of unconscious trauma energy is to clear all the conscious and subconscious energy regarding a specific imbalance first. Then sit and ask of Divine Beings in partnership with you in the Sacred Healing and Wisdom Circle, what unconscious and supra-conscious sources of energy are also contributing to some of the following; anxiety, chronic knee pain, feelings of doom, inability to find a mate, or your nightmares. Listen and know that you will get a sense of what that could be.

The answer may come through something you read, through dreams, through an email or a friend, or other ways besides directly hearing the guidance. However, after a lot of experience of asking and clearing unconscious and supra-conscious energies, after asking for help, you may eventually just come to a knowing of the specific unconscious stuck energy contributing to the imbalance you want to heal. Keep asking until you are able to imagine what the unconscious energy might be. It is worth the attention and patience.

If you have created new sources of unconscious or supra-conscious trauma energies in your present lifetime, you add them to unhealed unconscious energies that were never healed in this dimension previously. Unconscious and supra-conscious trauma energy just grows and grows until you command it out of your field. Therefore, there is usually a large backlog of unconscious or supra-conscious trauma energy when you first address this type of energy. All blocked energies taken on or created while in body have to be cleared here while you are in body once again.

During a session, if clearing is done at the unconscious or supra-conscious level, there is usually very little if any detox. That is because the imbalance resides in the unconscious and soul body rather than in the physical body so detox is usually minor. At the same time, clearing of unconscious and supra-conscious trauma energy can be between five and 35 times stronger than clearings for blocked conscious energy in terms of the intensity and depth of the healing.

In my experience, the following unconscious and supra-conscious blocked energies are the most frequently encountered: guilt, judgment, forgiveness, anger or rage, shame, fear, grief, self-worth, ego, control, doubt, desire, pride, family, abuse, abandonment, betrayal, mistrust, apathy, death, violence, war, loss, success, failure, financial, stress, racism, religious persecution, sexual, gender, punishment, attack, protection, regret, ethnic persecution, and tribulation.

Less frequently encountered, but still common unconscious and supra-conscious blocked energies include: anxiety, time, body, blame, tension, safety, disease (or specific disease), sacrifice, birth, protection, integrity, feeling unwanted, self-love, marriage, hate, aging, rejection, reputation, slave, misogyny, sexual preference, denial of the sacred, father or mother, wife or husband, partner, sibling, child, infertility, cancer, and heart.

I only find the following unconscious and supra-conscious blocked energies occasionally: image, subjugation, legacy, food, body image, drama, tension, entitlement, security, trepidation, refugee, prison, public image, drug, alcohol, obesity, drowning, starvation, poisoning, assassination, suffocation, germ, murder, vow, remorse, personal violence

For each imbalance above, you would express the imbalance as unconscious and/or supra-conscious [type of block energy from the list] trauma energy and all symptoms. Here are some more specific examples:

- A woman suffering from life-long claustrophobia was guided to clear for unconscious prison trauma energy.
- A man suffering from chronic insomnia was guided to clear for unconscious safety trauma energy.
- A woman suffering from left knee trauma including surgery, torn meniscus, and continual pain was guided to clear for unconscious father trauma energy.
- A man suffering from allergies was guided to clear for unconscious and supra-conscious security trauma energy.
- A man with recurring violent dreams was guided to clear for unconscious and supra-conscious violence and war trauma energies.
- A woman who spent her life being late to everything and feeling stressed was guided to clear for unconscious time trauma energy.
- A woman whose husband was completely closed to Divine Energy of any kind called for the healing of her husband for unconscious and supra-conscious denial of the sacred trauma energy.
- A man, who by self- report was quick to anger, was guided to clear for unconscious and supra-conscious shame and blame trauma energy.

You may wonder, did their imbalances clear up? In all the cases I have given here, these people's imbalances have come into balance. However, this was not the only work these individuals had done. Each of them had been clearing blocked energy in their own conscious and subconscious fields for a couple of years before they actually began clearing at the unconscious and supra-conscious levels.

The work begins where you are, with the imbalances you know about that are staring you in the face. All the guilt, anger, blame, judgment and un-forgiveness you know you carry needs to be cleared first before you can effectively tackle unconscious or supra-conscious trauma energies. The conscious imbalances we carry need to be cleared from our conscious mind first before the unconscious imbalances can be fully cleared.

If you still actively hate your boss, criticize your spouse, spew loud hateful energy, hold self-hateful thoughts, abuse substances, lie to others, cut yourself, or feel depressed, you must first clear the blocked energy and sources at conscious and subconscious levels, manifesting as these imbalances. It is a first order principle. You may not effectively skip over your own conscious imbalances and go to the unconscious sources and expect to be successful. However, in using the Six-Step Spiritual Healing Protocol, you will be guided to clear for consciously known imbalances at all levels of consciousness and in this way, you are beginning to clear at both the unconscious and supra-conscious levels from the beginning of your healing work.

In our conscious lives, we are responsible for making conscious and subconscious choices to hate, blame or judge others. This is where we need to begin to have a chance to eventually get to the underlying sources of imbalance at the unconscious or supra-conscious levels.

## UNDERSTANDING DIVINE HEALING ENTITY GROUPS

Healing Entity Groups refer to groups of Divine Beings who are out of body and committed to working with humans in this dimension throughout our lives. You do not usually find these beings or begin to effectively work with them until you have sought this type of healing support for yourself and others. The basics of this are tied to Free will.

If you want to live this life without any help, you can do that. If you choose to ignore everything about the Greater Whole, you can do that as well. If however, you would welcome Divine Healing support, guidance and healing, you can ask for that to manifest in your life and it will.

This happens provided you do not carry any blocked energy to this request at the conscious, subconscious, unconscious or supra-conscious (soul) level. Sometimes it is necessary to clear for all blocked energies affecting your ability to work with and receive Divine Spiritual healing at the physical level.

This can be brought about by stating something like the following; *I call forth the Violet/Sacred/Eternal Flame within me to consume all conscious, subconscious, unconscious and supra-conscious blocked energies manifesting as my inability to effectively work with Divine Entities, and receive support and healing from these Entities in appropriate ways for me. My intention is to work in Divine/Sacred intentional partnership towards healing for myself, for others and for our planet. And so it is.*

You may have heard of John of God also known in Portuguese as Joao de Deos whose healing center is located in Abadiania, Brazil. Thousands of people from all over the world come weekly for healing experiences to this healing center. There are a number of Divine Beings regularly present whose energy enters into Joao's body in order to bring healing to those visiting the healing center.

John of God is known as an unconscious medium. The life healing experienced in Abadiania is extraordinary in the human experience. There are surgeries taking place where actual stitches appear on a person's body but no hand is seen putting the stitches in the person. Others receive physical hands on healing of a seemingly painful procedure who never feel any pain. There are thousands of healing stories such as these available to those seeking this type of healing support.

When I visited Abadiania for three weeks, my intention was to learn to distinguish the various Divine Entities from one another. That was my stated goal. As I began to tune into the experience of sitting in sacred current, I learned to tell the Entities from one another. As years have passed, I have begun to work in deep relationship with the thousands of other Divine Entities who do not necessarily manifest energetically in this dimension but who are always available for the asking.

Thus far, I know of three groups of Divine Healing Entities who work directly with human healing as needed. The first group I came in contact with is referred to as the Casa Healing Entities with over 63,000 Divine Beings at the time of this writing. They serve humans physically and globally in this dimension and are generally located over Brazil. The second group is the Himalayan Healing Entities with over 86,000 Divine Beings serving the entire globe but are physically located over the Himalayan Mountains. The third group is the Bhutan Healing Entities with over 97,000 Divine Beings located over Bhutan but serving globally.

The Casa Healing Entities are organized physically over Brazil and work closely with the Abadiania Healing Center where Joao works most of the time. The other two groups are also physically centered over different parts of our globe as indicated. However, the services of each of these groups can be used by anyone living anywhere. I was directed recently to work more specifically in name with these Divine Healing Entities to enable me to call in continuous healing and spiritual healing support for humans that could be instantaneously received.

In one case, I was working with a woman who was manifesting organ and tissue cancer. I began my work with her by opening Sacred Space and then asked which group would be the most helpful and what level would be the best match for this person. I was led to work with the Himalayan Healing Entities, level eight for her specific issues along with the Angels of human organs and tissues. This work proceeded without my continually checking in to see if more healing energy was required. After four weeks of this healing support being called, all areas where cancer had been indicated, had disappeared. After we got that indication, she had medical tests done to confirm that she had no more cancer in her organs or tissues.

These groups of Healing Entities are organized by expertise and specialty level just as you might find in a hospital. So, for physical pain due to a seriously bruised toe, I recently called for Himalayan Healing Entity intervention for my toe, level three. When I woke up in the morning, there was almost no pain and no bruising at all evident. I was able to take a two-hour yoga class with no noticeable pain. From years of experience, I know that my body would often take three or four days before I could even consider taking a yoga class after such a serious bruise. The body still needs time to heal but the speed and total recovery is much quicker when working with Divine Healing Entities.

The breadth of the potential support is beyond anything I had every thought might be possible. Recent work with two people with glaucoma was very amazing. The guidance given for both clients was to call for transmutation healing energy to enable the damaged eye cells to change form, from damaged eye cells to healthy whole eye cells. While this was going on, one client said that she immediately had a clearing of her eye that was the most damaged and that the cloudy symptoms had gone away. The second client reported that when she went for medical tests after our healing, her eye pressure was down six to eight points. This is a work in progress so the complete outcome is not yet known.

There are other Divine Healing Entity groups who attend to different types of healing. There is one group of Divine Healing Entities over Washington D.C. who work with organizations, groups and organizational life of all kinds. This is the group I work with when I receive a call to work with a specific government, an economy, a start up or even a terrorist group.

There is a group over Ottawa, Canada working with Life Change issues of all kinds including moves, divorces, adoptions, new jobs, losing jobs, loss of housing, marriages, preparing for passing over, and many other life change issues.

There are three other groups, over Thailand, Ethiopia and Qatar concerned with Earth Changes, such as earthquakes, tsunamis, hurricanes, volcanic eruptions, grazing lands, droughts, rising waters, pollution, and climate change.

There are two groups of Divine Healing Entities over Aruba and New Zealand who work with sea creatures. There are groups of Divine Healing Entities over Botswana and Kazakhstan who work with animals. There is a group of Divine Healing Entities over the Galapagos Islands working with turtles, birds and insects. My understanding is that there are over 5.4 million Divine Healing Entities working with our globe, at the time of this writing, organized by types of expertise, indicated by levels. This number grows daily especially as we work with these Entities worldwide. As we all begin to work with Divine Beings for global healing, more and more Beings are available for working together in partnership. I have discovered a few of these Healing Entity Groups listed above. No doubt there are other groups that will continue to be revealed as needed.

## WORKING WITH DIVINE HEALING ENTITY GROUPS

It is advantageous to work with Divine Healing Entity Groups because some of these Beings have been in body and have expertise specific to our human, earth, atmosphere, plants, insects, birds, and animal conditions. Further, All Divine Beings working with us have willingly agreed to serve this Earth and all humans, plants, and animals living here regardless of whether they have been in body here or not.

When you call on these specific groups, you are working with the Greater Whole, known by many names including, Yahweh, God, Allah, The Beloved, Elohim, Great Spirit, The I AM Energy, The Great Oneness, etc. Every part of our being is connected to this Whole energy.

God Energy is always constant in its presence and glory. It is the pure loving Wholeness from which we all have been created, in the Image of All That Is. You can "talk to God" anytime you desire to do so. You are always heard. You are already part of that God Energy, all the time, in every situation. God is within and you are always connected.

Calling on Divine Source/God/The Oneness outside of yourself is not as effective as working in partnership with specific resources for calling forth healing. It is more effective to work in partnership with the available Divine Beings to bring about the desired changes you seek within yourself and with our unbalanced Earthly situations. You are a Divine Being having human experience. Thus, whatever you call forth for spiritual healing in your human form is coming from your Eternal Divinity.

Some of what is being presented here has been known to various religious traditions throughout all ages. From a particular religious path, you may know of a few Divine Beings such as a saint, a sage, a prophet, a divine leader, or an ancestor you can call to for help. Actually though, there are millions of Divine Beings available to help you when you call forth their energy, expertise and presence. Anyone can access those serving in this capacity by working with Healing Entities and accessing them through Silence.

## ACCESSING DIVINE ENTITY HEALING SUPPORT

Each person gets information via Divine Source in different ways. Therefore, use the most specific information you can obtain in calling forth support and healing from the Divine Healing Entities. I am sharing an approach here that anyone can use to work with these Entities regardless of the level of specific information you have available to you.

The first major understanding needed in working with Divine Healing Entities is that it is your responsibility to do your own work for clearing blocked energies you know you carry that may be manifesting as the imbalance you are interested in addressing. If you do not do your own work to clear as completely as you can, your ability to receive the healing of those in partnership with you will be diminished.

For example, I worked with a person who had a long history of depression with varying symptoms including poor sleep, emotional turmoil, and a sense of hopelessness. Before we could seek further support with Healing Entities, we needed to exhaust our own resources first. In our sessions, we called for specific clearings including gene-induced depression trauma energy, fear of always being depressed, fear of addiction to drugs, and a sense of separation and abandonment from God. These areas were each addressed and at some point all those topics we knew about had been addressed and identified, resolved, and rebalanced. There were still bouts of depression however, that triggered old response patterns again.

One day in Sacred Space together, it was given that we needed to clear these same areas at the subconscious, unconscious and supra-conscious levels so that all this old energy was completely clear from the entire field. We were working in Sacred Space, and the steps were given as to how this work should be done. Eventually, the depression episodes got shorter and less intense but they were still present.

One of the last things we addressed had to do with the residual imbalance in the body itself. The pituitary gland and the corpus callosum in the brain were out of balance with All That Is. We eventually were led to this information. All the previously blocked energy had manifest as an imbalance in the general brain itself. We needed another order of specific expertise to work with these imbalances.

We called in a specific level of the Himalayan Healing Entity support for the pituitary gland and the corpus callosum to be rebalanced in the brain. It is a joy to know that we can call healing so that the body can heal totally and completely. Several other similarly huge steps were given for healing work assisted by Divine Healing Entities and eventually this person went off drugs related to depression and is happily living symptom free.

These stories are shared to indicate that all that is needed is given in a Divine healing process. With most situations of imbalance, you do not start out knowing the total path that is needed for all the healing to manifest. Each step is given. The human part of this is to keep returning to the Divine-human partnership for the healing, even when the experiences seem to be indicating little or no lasting effect. You can use the Six-Step Spiritual Healing Protocol as one proven way to access Divine dialogue and these partnership opportunities.

## DIVINE VIBRATIONAL INTERVENTION

Divine vibrational intervention is a spiritual alternative for human physical treatment or surgery. The major prerequisite for this healing to be effective is that the person receiving it needs to be open to Divine vibrational intervention. Sometimes a person thinks it would nice to receive such healing, but energetically the person is not able to receive this type of healing for some unknown reason. The person seeking the Divine vibrational intervention is sometimes not even aware of this situation because the blocks are either in the subconscious, unconscious or supra-conscious level and are not known to the individual.

Sometimes when calling in energy for another, a self-defensive energetic sense is indicated from that person when they are not receiving that energy. The energy feels blocked or repelled. If such blocked energy exists, it can be cleared at the time of the intervention. The Six-Step Spiritual Healing Protocol can be used to clear all blocked energies manifesting as "Divine vibrational intervention trauma energy and all the symptoms". Then, the Divine vibrational intervention can continue and be received.

Divine vibrational intervention involves calling in specific Divine surgeons and healers from Divine realms for physical, emotional, mental or spiritual healing with an individual. Some of the successful vibrational interventions I have participated in include healing for bone and bone marrow cancer, liver, gallbladder, misaligned body parts, pancreatitis, intestinal and uterine tumors, knee imbalances, coronary valves, spinal discs, arteries, cysts, eye disorders, mental disorders, torn ligaments, hip flexors, muscles and tendons, hip dysplasia, and dissipation of blood clots. I imagine that any type of physical intervention needed could theoretically be effectively addressed in this way.

The process for Divine vibrational intervention begins with the Six-Step Spiritual Healing Protocol. The basic healing protocol prepares the energy fields of those involved. In other words, blocked energy manifesting as the specific physical imbalance, needs to be addressed before full physical healing can be achieved.

The first step is to clear all unseen blocked energy. The second step is to call for Divine vibrational intervention at the physical level. If blocked energies exist in the unseen levels, which are contributing to the specific imbalance, the body cannot heal fully until these issues are cleared. The call for Divine vibrational intervention can then follow the clearing of all blocked energies. The following case explores a Divine vibrational intervention.

A client in her 60s suddenly began to have severe pain in her hip. She had to use Epsom salt baths two times a day along with essential oils and ibuprofen to address the pain. The pain went on for about 10 days when it was revealed that she needed immediate hip intervention due to congenital hip dysplasia. She had been aware of the hip imbalances her whole life but the sudden onset of the pain required immediate attention.

In Silence, it was revealed that she needed Divine vibrational intervention to repair the imbalance in the bones and joint of the hip. The diagnosis was given as hip dysplasia. A Divine vibrational intervention was indicated and a Sacred Healing and Wisdom Circle was opened. There was clearing for blocked energies both for hip dysplasia trauma energy and for subconscious and unconscious gestational hip dysplasia trauma energy and all symptoms. This was followed by a call for Divine orthopedic surgeons to work in this physical dimension on the hip.

She was in a reclined position and the initial intervention took about fifteen minutes. During that time, the space for the healing vibrations was held in partnership for the client with the Divine Beings in the Sacred Healing and Wisdom Circle. As the intervention progressed, the client was aware of sensations in the hip but no pain or discomfort was experienced. When the intervention was completed for that day, it was revealed that she would receive hourly Divine healing pulsating vibrations until such time as the bones of the hip joint fully healed. She was to refrain from walking for three days. She could then slowly walk for 15 minutes adding five minutes a day. After four weeks, the hip was completely healed with the client was able to resume strenuous exercise as she had done before.

Another physical intervention was with a young woman in her 40s. She had four blocked heart arteries and an imbalance in the cardiac mitral valve. The session began with the Six-Step Spiritual Healing Protocol to open Sacred Space and clear for subconscious and unconscious heartbreak trauma energy and all symptoms including heart artery and mitral valve imbalances. All blocked energy was rebalanced. When this occurred, it was given that Divine vibrational intervention was required.

Two Divine cardiac surgeons were called in for the Divine vibrational intervention. The intervention took about 12 minutes and all four major cardiac arteries were addressed, as was the mitral valve in this session. No discomfort or pain was felt though sensations in the heart area were experienced. Continuous healing was indicated, as needed. Therefore this continuous healing was called in until all four arteries and the mitral valve were completely in Right Relationship with All That Is.

This process took nine days to complete. During the first day after the intervention, the client had some discomfort and slight pain. She had been instructed during the original healing intervention to keep her hand on her heart if this occurred and the sensations lasted about 15 minutes. She did feel more tired than usual for the first three to four days after the intervention. When the healing of the body was complete, she reported greater energy than before the intervention. Also her blood pressure was lower than before the intervention.

Divine vibrational intervention is the easiest way to describe what is happening with the body. The Divine vibrational interventions I have called forth have consisted of the Divine surgeons and healers raising the energy of specific cells to changes their form or function. Divine physical interventions raise the energetic vibrations within the body to such levels that the actual tissues themselves transform and heal, or the function of the tissues is changed or both things occur.

Early in learning to work with this energy, I called for Divine vibrational intervention with a tumor and thought it was being dissolved. In fact, the margins around the tumor were being cleared so that it could be completely taken out through human surgery and not require radiation or chemotherapy. In other words, what I thought was needed was not actually correct but the physical intervention occurred and exactly what was needed was given through Divine Knowing.

We as humans are always learning how to work with Divine Energy. Further, we are not responsible for the healing that is given. All Divine healing is completely guided and given though Divine Source and the most appropriate channels even if we do not fully understand the full extent of the intervention. Our calling forth this energy is sufficient for that which is needed.

## CONTINUOUS HEALING AND INCREASING RATES

Regardless of any of the above healing modalities being used, there is a possibility that continuous pulsating healing vibrations may be needed to ensure full healing. The physical body is very dense and slow to change as compared to the density of the energy that makes up the spiritual or the mental bodies. The unseen bodies such as the mental body and the spiritual body vibrate at higher frequencies than the dense physical body. For example, healing for the spiritual and thermal bodies can be received almost instantly. However, that healing energy has to work its way through all energetic layers of the entire energy field of the body before it manifests in the healing of the physical body. This can be challenging to wait for at times.

It is my experience that whenever healing is called for and received at the unseen body, it is eventually received in the physical body. All the symptoms of imbalance whether physical, mental, emotional, or spiritual, will heal as healing energy works its way through the levels of the entire body to the physical body itself, which is the last to receive the spiritual healing, in most cases.

Sometimes instantaneous healing is given and received at the level of the physical body when healing is called. Though all healing can be called in the same way, instantaneous healing sometimes manifests by the beneficence of Divine Source.

I can be working with a client who needs Divine vibrational intervention and receive the indication that continuous interventions are also needed. Continuous Divine vibrational intervention can be set up to continue on a divinely determined basis, until such time as the physical body can fully manifest the healing. In such cases, the person receiving the healing and the Divine Beings holding the space for the healing agree to this arrangement. No other human is needed to call in further specific treatments. The healing intervention energy is given as a result of calling for *continuous vibrational healing* during the initial healing experience.

When calling in any kind of continuous healing process, there may be an indication given that the healing process can be sped up for the person with the imbalance. When this is indicated, it is in Right Relationship to call for an increase in the rate of healing. If you can listen to the guidance given, you can frequently get a specific level of increase in the speed of normal healing that is desirable. When you have a sense of the rate of healing increase, you can call it forth.

You can say something similar to the examples in the Six-Step Spiritual

Healing Protocol, Chapter Seven in the step where you maximize the Healing. Refer to that section for additional information.

*I call forth an eight-fold increase in the normal healing rate for the balancing of my finances (or healing of my relationship with [name of person], forgiveness of myself, healing of my cancerous cells, etc.) trauma energy and all symptoms.*

If you are not able to determine a specific increase in the rate of healing needed, you can always call for the most expedient rate of healing possible.

*I call forth the most expedient rate of healing to manifest, for all imbalances and desired outcomes.*

## DIVINE STELLAR HEALING ENERGY

Divine Stellar energy, used here refers to energy originating from light giving bodies in the sky including the sun, moon and stars. This energy is sometimes referred to in the Bible as coming from the firmament, the sky above the earth. This energy differs from Divine physical intervention energy.

Divine Stellar healing energy is creation energy held in light producing sources themselves. These bodies of Light are made of the same chemical compounds as humans but as humans, we are in a different form. Therefore we share the same chemical building blocks of the sun, moon and stars and can use that Light energy for our healing.

You can call Divine Stellar energy to help any situation facing you physically, emotionally, mentally or spiritually. Also, this Energy is most effective with imbalances on our physical planet as well. It is appropriate to call for Divine Stellar healing energy for the following types of imbalances; cleaning up oil spills, invasive plants and fungi, epidemics, depression, addiction, pollution, lethargy, obesity, memory loss, and many other imbalances in this dimension. This energy was powerfully present with the recent epidemics of avian flu and the Ebola virus for example.

Using Divine Stellar energy and Divine physical vibrational intervention together is a powerful combination for healing. These forms of healing can be further enhanced with the energies of nutritious foods, as well. All food carries its own form of Divine Source energy.

Divine Source energy or vibrations of different kinds of meat differ from the vibrations of vegetables, which differ from the vibrations of grains and fruit. Each offers a different energy experience to the human body. This form of Divine Source energy comes under the auspices of Nature Intelligence, though Nature Intelligence is vastly more expansive than simply appearing in our food.

Nature Intelligence is another form of Divine Source energy that is contained within the forms of trees, plants, flowers, grasses, and found as well in wind, fire, earth, ethers, ice and water. Essential oils are a form of Nature Intelligence. Each oil possesses a unique vibration. When any aspects of Nature Intelligence healing sources are combined with both Divine Stellar healing and Divine vibrational healing, you have powerful combinations for healing. Explore all these possible combinations of Divine healing sources when imbalances show up.

All the following ways are effective in accessing Divine Stellar healing energy. Always work in a Sacred Healing and Wisdom Circle (see Six-Step Spiritual Healing Protocol) when calling this Divine Stellar healing energy forth. The pronoun *we* in these examples refers to you and the Divine Partners working with you.

*We call forth the Divine Stellar vibrational healing energy to support James in his healing from surgery (or in his physical healing from drug addiction, in the strengthening of his body from his accident, etc.)*

*We call forth Divine Stellar vibrational healing energy for Katherine for the healing of her emotions with her mother, (or for her suicidal thoughts, for her fear of violence, for her fear of the dark, etc.)*

*We call forth Divine Stellar vibrational healing energy to transform the phosphorus runoff forming toxic algae in Lake Erie and the Atlantic Ocean.*

*We call forth Divine Stellar vibrational healing energy for the rebalancing of my sweet gum tree that is showing signs of decay.*

Divine Stellar vibrational healing energy can be called into any situation where there is imbalance. Because this Light substance is so similar to our own chemical compounds though in different form, it is very compatible with our own beings. It is a unique type of energy that unconditionally supports healing whether the issues are emotional, mental, physical, self-protective, karmic, curse, doubt, or fear based. It is a source of healing energy that is easily accessible and always supportive of our healing.

In one instance, I was working with a person's eyesight. They had had good eyesight as an early teen but their eyes got progressively worse. We had worked with the normal trauma imbalances and blocked energies given and they still had imbalances in long distance vision. It was finally given for us to call for Divine Stellar Healing energy for their full healing of their long distance vision. At printing, this case is still manifesting healing of the vision but now this client can drive without glasses in the day and can go without lenses in her house with little need at all for lenses in the daytime.

# CHAPTER NINE

# Genetic and Gestational Imbalances

AFTER MANY YEARS OF HEALING using various adaptations of the Six-Step Spiritual Healing Protocol, I began to be increasingly aware of the times in which that healing approach was not totally sufficient. For example, I suffered with extreme spring allergies for over 30 years. I had tried all sorts of remedies from acupuncture and acupressure to prescription medications, and homeopathic preparations. I would clear for all types of allergies each year before spring allergies and some years were more successful than others. I would combine homeopathic medications with spiritual healing and might only be inside for four weeks instead of eight. If I started early before the first pollen, it might be only 10 days of truly feeling miserable even while taking medications and using a neti pot, a specific type of small mug designed to flush out nostrils.

I was still feeling deeply affected by allergies every year. As I began to seek other ways of healing, I asked out loud one day in Sacred Space; "What is it that I am missing about my allergies"? I got that I needed to clear for these allergies at the gene level. Thus began an entirely new dimension of healing possibilities. I was guided to some of the latest scientific research on genes. That research is incorporated into healing protocols shared here and can be used to heal the gene-induced imbalances in our lives.

## GENE-INDUCED IMBALANCES

Recent scientific research is beginning to provide a new understanding of genetic inheritance based on epigenetics. Epigenetics studies how modifications are made to our DNA and how genes get "switched on or off" sometimes resulting in profound changes. Even more surprising is that these changes in DNA switches may be passed on from one generation to another. In a provocative documentary titled "Ghost In Your Genes" produced by the BBC and aired by PBS on NOVA, this was the summary of the emerging science.

> *At the heart of this new field is a simple but contentious idea – that genes have a 'memory'. That the lives of your grandparents – the air they breathed, the food they ate, even the things they saw – can directly affect you, decades later, despite your never experiencing these things yourself. And that what you do in your lifetime could in turn affect your grandchildren.*
>
> *The conventional view is that DNA carries all our heritable information and that nothing an individual does in their lifetime will be biologically passed to their children. To many scientists, epigenetics amounts to a heresy, calling into question the accepted view of the DNA sequence – a cornerstone on which modern biology sits.*
>
> *Epigenetics adds a whole new layer to genes beyond the DNA. It proposes a control system of 'switches' that turn genes on or off – and suggests that things people experience, like nutrition and stress, can control these switches and cause heritable effects in humans.[12]*

Further research covered in the documentary focused on the long historical records of a Swedish town for births, deaths, and food harvests that went back hundreds of years.

> *At first, they found that life expectancy of grandchildren was directly affected by the diet of the grandparents. Fatal childhood diabetes was often associated with their father's father living during a period of reduced food supply. In a further development, the records revealed that triggering of a trans-generational effect was dependent upon the time in the grandparents' lives when food had been in short supply. For the grandfather it was just before puberty and for the*

*grandmother it was the moment of conception, crucial moments in the development of sperm and egg. These observations suggest that environmental information, in this case supply of food, was being imprinted on the DNA of the sperm and egg, providing strong evidence that epigenetic inheritance occurs in humans.[13]*

I have found that there are direct parallels in my spiritual healing work. If a mother is starving when pregnant, there will be genetic inheritance of a starvation imprint passed. This can manifest in numerous ways in the child from failure to thrive to obesity.

If a male is, for example, severely beaten or abused just before puberty, there will be energetic imprints in his genes connected to this history as well. This could manifest as intimidation, fear of violence, bullying, aggressive physical behaviors or as a range of other manifestations. Understanding when gene-induced imbalances are present is the most challenging aspect of addressing these issues.

Though these manifestations go beyond the current science of epigenetics, they have been confirmed many times in Sacred Space and in actual cases. In this spiritual healing work, clearing needs to occur at both the genetic and epigenetic levels for a full healing of any gene-induced imbalance.

Some of the types of situations rebalanced using clearing for gene-induced imbalances include, obesity, depression, anxiety, addiction, allergies, heart disease, cancer, memory loss, insomnia, acne, vision, mental thought patterns, hearing loss, nightmares, panic attacks, etc. Some gene-induced imbalances include more complex issues such as resistance to Mother Earth energy, trust of the Universe, cardiac trust, stranglehold of the mind, inability to bond, body image, mistrust of being in body, ability to thrive to name a few.

Many first order imbalances, meaning originating from this lifetime may have hereditary line blocked energy but that is different from gene imbalances. Hereditary line blocked energy means that the situation was experienced energetically through the environment of one's previous years. For example, you may carry the fear of poverty from growing up with severely limited financial resources in the present lifetime. Or, you may carry gene-induced fear of poverty at the gene level passed through generations, originating from before this particular lifetime. This genetic level of imbalance is more deeply entrenched than when the imbalance is a first order imbalance and not gene related.

Gene-induced imbalances mean that you have received genes causing imbalance during the gestation process. These "detracting genes" carry a particular energetic imprint that can manifest as imbalances at some time in one's life. These detracting genes must be turned off or neutralized at the genetic and epigenetic levels to be able to completely rebalance and become life-enhancing genes.

It is possible to have imbalances that need to be cleared at the basic level, using our Six-Step Spiritual Healing Protocol, and also need further clearing at the genetic and epigenetic levels. This is a useful area to explore when you are not able to fully heal.

When I first asked how to bring full healing to these more challenging situations, I was led to videos. The videos explored specific generational human experiences and new gene research shared in footnote 9. I was trained through Silence while in a meditative state, over several weeks, in calling forth gene- induced healing for various imbalances.

One way to identify a gene-induced imbalance is to determine if the condition in question has been chronic. For example, if a person seems to have had an addiction to alcohol from their early years, this may well be a gene-induced imbalance. Alternatively though, the imbalance could stem from the situation in which the person now in question was raised. If abuse of alcohol was present when the addicted person was raised, alcohol abuse trauma energy needs to be considered along with a possible gene-induced imbalance.

Unbalanced energy before seven years of age can leave subconscious and unconscious imprints in our fields that manifest later in life. Before seven years of age, we are generally not fully conscious. Therefore, what happens then can remain with us for our whole life without our understanding where it came from, until addressed and re-balanced. When issues later in life seemingly arise from nowhere, they can have roots before we were seven years of age. These types of issues are not those we are focused on here, even though they can be equally challenging to identify.

For gene-induced imbalances identified through Divine Knowing, personal intuition or as a hunch, the specific genes need to be addressed directly so that they can be neutralized. For all gene-induced imbalances, we begin with the Six-Step Spiritual Healing Protocol in Chapter Seven that includes clearing at the hereditary line (first order clearing) and continues with the following clearings from the genetic and epigenetic levels if those clearings are insufficient.

To clear for Gene-Induced Imbalances, Use the Six-Step Spiritual Healing Protocol as shared above with the following changes:

1. State the trauma energy as a specific gene-induced imbalance and all symptoms (e.g., gene-induced depression trauma energy and all symptoms, gene- induced fat holding energy and all symptoms, etc.)

2. Use the Six-Step Spiritual Healing Protocol to clear all blocked energies and where they reside as indicated. Then add, *Clear all blocked energies at the genetic and epigenetic levels manifesting as gene-induced pollen allergy (or name the imbalance) trauma energy and all symptoms.*

3. Specify that healing is to include all genes contributing to this imbalance by either stating the specific number of genes involved or by simply saying, *this is for rebalancing all genes contributing to gene-induced sleep apnea (name the imbalance) trauma energy and all symptoms in the energetic and physical field.*

4. Maximize the healing. *I call for Level 9 Himalayan Healing Entities (level 9 Casa Healing Entities or level 10 Bhutan Healing Entities) to work at the physical level to bring about rebalancing of the gene(s) to manifest balance within the physical and energetic fields.*

5. If full healing for the client is not received the first time around, there may be too many genes to be all addressed at the same time. Repeat this same process until all symptoms subside.

## GENE-INDUCED PANIC ATTACKS

Over 90% of the healing approach I use has been given in Sacred Silence and through trial and error. Therefore, the toughest situations would show up for me when I was apparently ready to learn more about the area I had been working in for some months. In working with panic attacks, for example, there are all manner of imbalances that can be identified and cleared on the path to freedom from these attacks.

Some of the work with those experiencing panic attacks often pointed to violent trauma, abuse trauma, fear of violation, belittling trauma energy, victim trauma energy to name a few areas that have been indicated for healing. These areas were spiritually given or "tagged" if you will because they contributed to panic attacks in a particular person. Healing would be given and received and then we would see what happened.

My clients often referred to panic attacks as anxiety coming out of nowhere. Just as often as a person might have a glimpse of what was behind the attacks, others would have no clue at all about why these attacks had suddenly started. All expressed the sensation of a sudden rush of adrenaline that lasted varying amounts of time with a range of consequences for the client.

After working with several people with anxiety for several months, I was feeling that I was missing something major that could help them. I asked Divine Source what I was missing one day with regard to panic attacks and was guided to gene-induced panic attacks. In these situations, individuals literally have received genes that contribute to having panic attacks. When asked if either parents or grandparents manifest panic attacks, there was often knowledge of this having been present for their ancestors and sometimes with siblings as well. This opened up an entirely new avenue for addressing panic attacks.

When asking about gene-induced conditions, I ask for how many genes are involved in manifesting the imbalance we are working with. I am given a number and proceed as follows.

To clear for gene-induced panic attacks:

1. Use the Six-Step Spiritual Healing Protocol and call for clearing of gene-induced panic attack trauma energy and all symptoms.
2. Determine how many genes are involved, if possible or call for all involved genes to be addressed.
3. Call for the rebalancing for the 3 (or another number) of genes that are contributing in any way to gene-induced panic attack trauma energy and all symptoms.
4. Call for the rebalancing of each gene to take place at the genetic and epigenetic level.

5. Repeat the call until all genes come into Right Relationship with All That Is.

Sometimes there is only one call needed for this healing and all the genes are rebalanced. In other situations, there have to be separate calls for each gene involved in the manifestation of panic attacks. I label them gene 1, gene 2, gene 3, etc. Many other imbalances that the individual may be dealing with such as a disease, medications, or emotional imbalances can be intertwined with gene-induced panic attacks.

In one case, after clearing for gene-induced panic attacks was complete, my client no longer needed the medications she was taking. In another case, a client was holding onto a belief at the unconscious level that she could never be fully well. This needed to be cleared before all the genes could be brought into full healing.

## GESTATIONAL IMBALANCES

Gestational imbalances are imbalances taken on in the baby's body and energetic field while still in the mother's body. This can be due to an energetic exchange from the mother to the child while in utero. This may also be due to imbalances in the fertilization process that manifest during gestation. The presenting imbalances may include the following: an unwanted pregnancy, a depressed (or grieving, malnourished, anxious, abused, ill) mother, a financial or energy draining pregnancy, a wartime pregnancy, etc. The energetic environment of the pregnant mother can remain in the child's energy field and manifest in countless ways throughout the child's life.

I have worked with several adults, who knew that their mothers had lost a child in birth less that one year before their mother became pregnant again with the second child, my clients. For one client, in Sacred Space, it was indicated that at pregnancy, this mother was both grieving the loss of her previous baby and anxious about this new baby and about the pregnancy itself. When we checked, my client was carrying gestational depression and gestational desire to be loved. This meant during her time in utero, she received these feelings as they passed across the placenta.

My client in present day by her own description was suffering from chronic depression and acute feelings of needing to know repeatedly that she was loved. This manifested as feeling vulnerable, confused and unsuccessful in close relationships, feeling ungrounded in many decisions, feeling depressed about her life and direction, feeling estranged with her mother as well as feeling hopeless.

When the healing for gestational depression trauma energy and gestational desire to be loved trauma energy were both cleared from her energy field, the severity of these symptoms lifted and allowed her to make self recognized progress with her depression and with intimate relationships.

Another group case involved several women who had each experienced years of challenging issues regarding insufficient funds for their lives. It was given that each was carrying gestational abundance trauma energy that was manifesting as years of feeling concern around having steady work, unstable success with attracting clients and a sense of worry and burden regarding money. Each client's mother had carried these same issues when each of the now adult women was in utero. This clearing for gestational abundance trauma energy at the conscious, subconscious, unconscious and supra-conscious levels was part of their individual work towards creating greater ease and grace with abundance in their lives.

Clearing for gestational imbalances can alleviate a myriad of imbalances that may have been present for one's entire life. An example of how to phrase gestational imbalances for clearing, follows.

Begin by using the Six-Step Spiritual Healing Protocol in Chapter Seven to prepare for clearing of this blocked energy. Use the following phrasing for gestation trauma energy. Select one of these blocked energies listed below or substitute you own wording for the imbalances you want to be cleared from your energy field. After this work is done for yourself, you can extend the healing to your mother whether she is alive or passed and she will not have to do that healing herself again if ever in this dimension in the future.

To clear for gestational imbalances:

1. Use the Six-Step Spiritual Healing Protocol and identify the imbalance being addressed for clearing of gestational trauma energy and all symptoms.

2. Call for clearing for gestational rage (or depression, feeling unwanted, feeling unimportant, fear of having no voice, feeling ignored, anxiety, desire to be loved, stress and tension, hopelessness, abundance, insomnia, fear of being attacked, fear of being in body, etc.) trauma energy and all symptoms at the conscious, subconscious, unconscious and supra-conscious levels. Repeat this healing again until there is no indication of this gestational imbalance in the energy field.

3. Continue with the Six-Step Spiritual Healing Protocol to complete this process.

# CHAPTER TEN

# Negative Spirits and Obsessions

THERE ARE MANY THOUSANDS OF SPIRITS all over the globe who have passed out of their bodies but have not passed into the Light as a permanent condition. These spirits stay in the Earth dimension for many reasons, including concerns over loved ones, fear of becoming non-existent, death shock, shame and un-forgiveness of self, blame and anger with others, etc. They continue to be present but without bodies. Some have simply not had a spiritual or religious ceremony that would have commended them to the Light and guided them in how to go to the Light and to their next destination.

There are a number of ways a spirit can remain in this dimension. Sometimes as these spirits go about their wanderings, they will see the Light in humans and will remain near these beings where they live and reside. If their presence can be known by a human with skills to send them to the Light, they will usually go when guided to do so and given a pathway for how to proceed.

In other instances, spirits who carry a great deal of darkness such as hatred, anger, and blame energy can energetically attach to a person in body who is carrying this same negative energy they are carrying. This can be disastrous for a human being because all his or her own negative thoughts and feelings are exacerbated by the additional energy of the negative spirit attachment. This can sometimes produce extreme consequences including deep depression and diagnoses of bi-polar disorders or other mental illnesses.

Whatever the reason for originally staying in this dimension, the place for every spirit is towards the Light, without exception. Regardless of attached spirits or simply ones in the environs, it is a huge support to the living and the dead to send these spirits to the Light. There is no future for them in this dimension.

When the spirits of loved ones remain in this dimension, it is most difficult for the remaining relatives in body to heal from the person's death. The spirit of the departed being can still feel present because it may well be right in the room with relatives. It is easier for loved ones remaining in this dimension to heal from death when the spirit of the departed individual passes into the other dimension of Light and Wholeness.

This work needs to be done in a Sacred Space opened by those responsible for casting the spirit to the Light. Whatever traditions are comfortable for doing that are fine. If none are personally familiar, you can always open Sacred Space as is done for the Healing Protocol to work with these Earth bound spirit beings.

Within Sacred Space, you need to determine if you are working with an unattached spirit being or an attached negative spirit being. For work with a negative spirit attachment, two things need to happen.

First, if the negative spirit is attached to a human being, the reasons for the attraction of the negative spirit attachment need to be cleared from the person's field. In this regard, the negative spirit attachment is a blessing in disguise because otherwise, the negative energies within the person would most likely remain unhealed. In this way, the person can be cleared of all the dark energies attracting a negative spirit attachment to self.

Secondly, the negative spirit attachment needs to be cast to the Light where the spirit can continue its eternal journey. When spirits remain in this dimension it is as if they are stalled in their eternal journey. There is no way to grow or learn in this dimension because the spirit is unable to interact in positive ways with the surroundings. They cannot be seen but by a very few humans with the gifts of second sight. They cannot be heard except by a very few humans gifted with second sound. The life of a negative spirit being in this dimension is basically marking time until that spirit energy is able to move into the Light and continue his or her eternal journey.

If you are working with an unattached spirit being, two possibilities for support are given. Sometimes, the spirit being simply needs to be cast to the Light. Especially when working with groups of unattached spirits, say for example those from a battlefield or from a country, the guidance can simply be to cast all those being to the Light. At times, I have worked with thousands of unattached spirit beings being cast at one time to the Light from a specific geographic area.

However, when working with a small group or an individual spirit, there may be guidance for clearing their blocked energies enabling those energies to literally drop to this dimension so that they do not carry those congested energies forward with them to the Light. This serves them well and if blocked energies are cleared here, they do not need to ever be cleared again unless it is for the purposes of teaching others how to do this work. After that clearing, the spirit beings need to be cast to the Light as well. Guidance as to how to proceed is readily given if you are called to this work.

Unattached spirit beings and attached negative spirits are best helped by enabling them to pass to the Light. In the early stages of doing this work, I asked whether I was to always assume that a spirit's place was toward the Light rather than remaining here perhaps with a human being who was depressed or ill, for example. I was given to understand that there was no question that all spirit beings are better going to the Light after they leave their bodies in this dimension.

When we leave our bodies, we are to always cross over to the Light in order to continue our eternal journeys. If a spirit chooses to stay here, knowingly or otherwise, that spirit is not progressing and has no chance to process the lessons has learned while in this lifetime. As stated earlier, loved ones find it much easier to heal from the loss of a dear one, when that person passes into the Light and energetically moves on with their own journeys. This has continued to be my experience with all those I have worked with through the years with their passing into the Light.

For all people, when we die, our place is towards the Light. We will be guided to the location where we are to process this lifetime, heal from it and restore our energies before we move onto our next calling. I have been repeatedly told, we continue on the other side in much the same way as we do here but without a physical body. Our interactions are more purely energy based than here but we each still have a soul calling us to our own true selves.

Therefore in all situations, when we assist others in going to the Light, we are helping others to reach their rightful locations with grace and ease.

Even those who have actually attached to another person due to their shared fears, darkness and anger belong on the other side, with the Light.

We will address two different categories of spirits in this section. There are unattached spirits who remain here for a wide range of reasons often roaming around. There are also spirits who have remained here after death and have become negative spirits attached to a human often causing exacerbated emotions and trauma energy for that person.

At one time, I experienced working with unattached spirits in a public parking lot. I had never caused a car accident in over 35 years of driving. I was parked in a parking lot where I regularly parked. One day, I backed out of my parking space and wrapped my front fender around an I-beam that I had parked beside for over 4 years, several times a week. I heard the crunch of the fender being smashed and I was simply astounded.

While I was waiting for the tow truck, I got the strangest feeling that there were some negative spirit energies in the parking garage. I opened Sacred Space and was told there were two imp-like spirit energies in the parking garage who had caused many accidents in the past three and half years. I had an image of them laughing raucously over my most recent accident. Using the protocol for unattached spirits, below, they were cast to the Light and the garage was restored to normal energy.

Another experience of an unattached spirit occurred when I was visiting a friend who had recently purchased an old house in the country. My friend was showing two of us around the house and upon entering a small room, she said that this room was where the ghost of the house lived. This ghost was apparently well known in the neighborhood as a legend and could be heard sometimes walking on the floor at night.

The story was that she had stayed in the house since the civil war because when she died very young, she was waiting for her loved one to return who had gone to war. We sat on the bed in the room and decided to hold the space for this "ghost" as she was referred to, to be cast to the Light. She did pass over into her eternal space. This felt right for the spirit though she had offered some sense of companionship to the owner who needed to first agree to sending the spirit to the Light, before that could be accomplished.

These are the sorts of situations you might encounter if called to work with unattached or attached spirits in this dimension. What always helped me when faced with these situations was the thought, "if not I, then who would help these spirits"? That gave me the courage I needed to try and be of service.

One needs to feel called to this type of work with spirits before undertaking it. It is not for all people. However, if you have a knowing or have ever had a knowing of the presence of spirits among us, this work could be for you. Perhaps you have shied away from that because of fear of the unknown or uncertainty about how to go about this. The steps given in this section can be used by all those called to this work. The way we actually command or cast spirits to the Light is the almost exactly the same whether they are attached to a human or not. More will be given about this later in this section.

## UNATTACHED SPIRITS

Unattached spirits are those who have not left this dimension when they died. They are here doing a wide range of things but not attaching to humans. Perhaps upon death, there was no direction as to how to proceed through the transition to the other side. Or perhaps the spirit had an expectation of being conscious after death. Spirits in this dimension may choose to remain because of un-forgiveness, guilt, fear or worry to name a few reasons for remaining. A spirit may have remained in the general vicinity of living loved ones while not actually attaching to a human. Sometimes, spirits have remained in a house or buildings where some trauma occurred or they are roaming through familiar locations but they are not bothersome or even known to humans. There are many variations in the way unattached spirits remain in this human realm.

My first experience working with an unattached spirit, when I began this work, was with a close relative, who had passed. I went into prayer the day after her passing, before any formal memorial or burial services and asked if there was any assistance I could give this person on her journey, not really knowing what to expect. Her spirit was still in this dimension at the time. I was led through a series of clearings specifically for her blocked energies held in her energy field, so that none of the imbalanced energies from her lifetime remained in her field, to travel with her soul from this dimension.

As the energies were called out for her, there was heavy residue of energy that fell to the Earth dimension each time another blocked energy was cleared from her energy field. When the work was complete, without my saying another word, she left this dimension in a flash of Divine Light that I saw in my mind's eye and was gone to the other side. I was astounded that this took place so orderly. I asked what had happened in Silence and received confirmation that she had indeed passed to the Light.

All anger, fear, guilt, blame, jealousy, loss, regret, and judgment that we heal in this dimension stays in this dimension. Further, all imperfect ways of thinking and acting, in fact, all imbalances we have ever carried, have to be healed in the dimension in which they originate. We have all the chances we need to clear all our imbalances, as we are all eternal. Therefore, when we help another clear their imbalances while still here, those imbalances do not require healing the next time they are in body. In this way, we can render a valuable service with any spirits we come in contact with, by helping all the old blocked energies still in their energetic field to be cleared.

In my own early experience, I was not able to actually discern a spirit presence in my general vicinity. I might get an indication through Silence but that ability to discern a spirit presence evolved over time. I did not know for many years that my father's energy had remained in our family home for 8.5 years between the time that he died and the time that my mother passed away. I eventually discovered this because their house would not sell for several years after my mother died. Our real estate agent actually told me that one afternoon while sitting quietly in the house, she felt a spirit presence who did not want the house to sell. I was called to attend to that situation the next day.

After that comment, I asked in Silence if my father's unattached spirit was in the house. I got "yes", he was in the family home. I went to the house to cast his spirit energy to the Light. In this case however, I needed to first clear for the anger and frustration I had that my father's energy had remained in this dimension and that his presence has made it impossible to sell the house for over 3 years after my mother had originally moved to a retirement center and then passed away. When all this blocked energy cleared, working in Sacred Space, we were able to cast his spirit energy into the Light. The house sold within two months.

Since that time many other similar situations have been identified and resolved often due to questions of why living spaces will not sell or due to reported sightings or unexplained phenomena in residences. Often, residences could not be sold because the energy in the house was being disturbed by a spirit presence. As said earlier, the place for all spirits is in the Light. As I developed more experience with spirit energies in partnership with Divine Beings, we were able to cast these spirits to the Light from long distances including from other countries.

Sometimes in working with unattached spirits, there is guidance given to clear for any remaining blocked energies keeping the spirit in this dimension or confounding his or her ability to go to the Light, as was the case with my relative. Clearing for specific blocked energies the spirit may be carrying will lighten his or her soul load by relieving them of these energies. These blocked energies could include shame, guilt, anger, fear, grief, pride, desire, regret, retribution, perceived need to protect, lack of knowledge about how to follow the Light, etc. After being here a long time, the same processes needed by humans are still very helpful for spirits stuck in this dimension as well.

There are other trauma energies that may be keeping a spirit in this dimension over a long period of time. These could include feeling responsible for leaving a loved one, worried about a person's ability to live their own lives without the spirit's presence or even just not wanting to completely leave loved ones and pass to the Light for any numbers of reasons. However, in all cases, everything cleared for an unattached spirit is something that will not follow the spirit into another incarnation, form or formless presence in the future.

Sometimes in working with unattached spirits, they just appear in our energy fields drawn by our Light. However in all cases, these spirits still need to be cast to the Light. As shared earlier, I was unable to discern when a negative spirit was in my house until someone was having nightmares or insomnia. As time went on, I did not feel this was a good experience, so I asked in Sacred Space for an indication of a negative unattached spirit be given to me so that I could send them to the Light without my family suffering their presence.

What began to happen was that I experienced immediate and strong headaches and that was the first way I knew that there was a spirit presence in my field. This was a good indication for me because I did not normally have headaches at all. So, it was a reliable indication of a spirit presence.

However, I did not like having severe headaches and after a few months of this, I asked for there to be another way I was informed of a spirit presence. Then I manifested a tightening of my upper chest as an indication of a spirit presence. This was easier for me but of course this differs with all humans, what will work. In the beginning I got severe tightening of the chest and that was too strong for me as well. So, over time, the means for communicating spirit presences was adjusted and became milder and milder as I readily recognized the spirit presence. In all cases, these spirits were cast to the Light after realizing they were present. There were numerous times over the years that a person visiting our house or coming as a client brought a negative spirit with them into our home. This was all very helpful in being trained in how to effectively work with spirit presences of all kinds.

## ATTACHED SPIRITS

Attached spirits are spirits who literally attach their dark energy to a human being's energy field. Because the attachment to a human is always negative, they are referred to here as negative spirits. There are three levels of negative spirit attachments that indicate the depth of the attachment to the human. The lowest to highest levels of attachment are as follows; negative spirit attachments, negative spirit obsession attachments, and negative spirit possession attachments. Each level indicates a greater level of entwinement with the human being. There is no question that each of these attachments is a negative occurrence for the human involved.

Basically, the negative spirit attaches to the familiar vibrations of a human who shares similar negative energetic imbalances. The spirit becomes focused on influencing and sharing types of darkness and imbalances with the human. A negative spirit's attachment to a human is a way to share familiar ground in this regard. A spirit attaches to human dark energy because it enables them to be more connected to life and energy than is otherwise available to them primarily because they do not belong here, in the first place. Any level of attachment prolongs the negative spirit's presence in this dimension and that is definitely not positive for the spirit or for humans in the long run.

The person who is experiencing a negative attachment at any level is subject to overwhelmingly negative feelings and emotions often without knowing what is happening for them. They often feel anxious, on edge, out of sorts, depressed and angry or all of these feelings together. Feelings and emotions are exacerbated beyond the person's normal levels of imbalance putting them at risk for injury, illness, hospitalization, insomnia, depression, nightmares, destruction and mayhem of enormous proportions. Even psychotic episodes can be the result of negative spirit attachments. I have known humans who are in a conscious process of clearing their own fears and anguish, who have purposely avoided going by both cemeteries and hospitals on their way through town, to lessen their chances of attracting a negative spirit attachment without meaning to.

It is possible for a person to attract more than one negative spirit attachment and at different levels of intensity. In these cases each negative spirit needs to be individually cast from the human's energy field. It is common for those who are regularly using illegal drugs, excessively drinking or gambling to attract negative spirit attachments because their energetic bodies are broadcasting these negative tendencies and addictions. These people then attract negative spirits who share these same addictions thus exacerbating all their addictive tendencies.

I frequently get called by clients who report feeling noticeably badly, wondering what is happening for them. This is a good indication for me that negative spirits might be present for them. As more and more work with negative or stuck spirits progressed, I found that it was possible to cast these spirits to the Light whether they were in the room with me or across an ocean from me. In every situation presented, I work in Sacred Space without fail. I do this to both protect myself and to work in partnership for the most effective outcomes.

My command for a spirit to go to the Light is one part of the equation and the other part is the presence of Angels and Divine Beings who hold the space for them to follow the Light to their destination. I personally never felt the slightest desire to try to do this on my own. I deeply value working in partnership with Divine Beings to accomplish this work.

## CASTING MULTIPLE NEGATIVE SPIRITS TO THE LIGHT

As my work with attached and unattached spirits continued, I was led to work with larger and larger numbers of spirits in far away places and always in Divine Partnership and Sacred Space. I remember two relatives calling me from overseas in different countries, at different times with stories of horrible nightmares for entire groups of people they were with as well as for themselves. This became a clear indication that unattached negative spirits in large numbers were being attracted to those visiting these places due to the Light in the group that certain individuals carried.

In one case, there were over thirty people having severely dark nightmares in a castle, every night. When the clearing was done for hundreds of spiritual presences stuck there, the nightmares stopped. In another location, unattached spirits from throughout an entire country were sent into the Light by the thousands. It was revealed that for many years, no form of sending spirits into the Light had been common among these people. There was a huge group of unattached spirits stuck in that country. These experiences led to three years of intense work with large numbers of unattached spirits needing to be sent to the Light from around the globe as indicated through Silence that, at that time, formed a major part of my global prayer work.

## CASTING ATTACHED NEGATIVE SPIRITS TO THE LIGHT

Speak aloud all italicized words, to give form and strength to the call in this dimension. If you cannot determine the type of the negative spirit, name all three types as you clear blocked energy and cast out the spirit.

1. *I open this Sacred Healing and Wisdom Circle to support me (or name person with spirit attachment). I welcome the Ascended Masters, the Angelic Host, the Cosmic Light Beings of the Universe, the Divas and Nature Intelligences and the Divine Healing Entities of highest Light from all traditions to partner with me today.*

2. *Sacred Flame within me (or name person with spirit attachment) come forth and clear all blocked emotional, mental, thermal, spiritual, hereditary line, karmic, curse and spell energies that have contributed to my (or the person's) attracting a negative spirit attachment (or negative spirit obsession attachment, negative spirit possession attachment).*

3. *Clear all blocked energy from the original source through all time and space, from cells in the body and from all memories and patterns memory at the conscious, subconscious, unconscious and supra-conscious levels.*

4. *Where these negative energies have resided within me (or name the person), we call in the Divine pure pink ray of Unconditional Love to transform the dark, low vibrating energies and to fill my (or the person's) body and energy field. Let this manifest. And So It is, Amen.*

5. *I call forth the Angelic Host to surround the negative spirit attachment (or negative spirit obsession attachment, negative spirit possession attachment) attached to me (or name the person).*

6. *I speak directly to the negative spirit attached to me (or name the person). You may not remain attached to me (or name the person). There is no future for you here. You must go now. Do not attach to any other sentient being in this dimension. Your future is towards the Light. Follow the Light. All is forgiven. Be not afraid. We send you with blessings and support. Go now. Do not remain here. Fear not! Follow the Light! All is well. Go now with the blessings of Divine Presence. And So It Is! Amen.*

7. *I give thanks for the presence of the Divine Beings working with me (or us) here today. And So It Is! Our deep gratitude, Amen.*

## CASTING UNATTACHED NEGATIVE SPIRITS TO THE LIGHT

Speak aloud all italicized words, to give form and strength to the call in this dimension.

1. *I open a Sacred Healing Space to support me, and the negative spirit in my house (or Sue and the negative spirit in her presence, the negative spirit in my friend Rachel's apartment, etc.). I welcome the Ascended Masters (or Jesus, Yogananda, Mother Mary, Shirdi Sai Baba, etc.) the Angelic Host, the Cosmic Light Beings of the Universe and the Divine Healing Entities of Highest Light who can partner with us today.*

2. *I call for the Angels to completely surround the unattached spirit in my basement (or in this living room, in Dora's garage, in Bob's attic, etc.)*

3. *I speak directly to the unattached spirit in my (or name the person) presence. You must go now! You cannot stay in this house or anywhere in this dimension. Your future is towards the Light. There is no future for you here. You may not remain here. Go to the Light. All is forgiven. You must go now. Do not hesitate. All is forgiven. There is no future for you here. Fear not! All is well! This is your chance. Follow the Light! Go now with the blessings of goodness and love. And so it is. Amen.*

4. *I give thanks for the presence of the Divine Beings helping and supporting this work today. And So It Is! Amen.*

## NEGATIVE OBSESSION PRESENCES

Negative obsession presences are a third type of negative energy that resides within the body or energy field of humans and animals. These obsession presences make it impossible to completely heal an area of the body. Typically, if we have had chronic pain, infection or imbalance in an area of the body, it is highly possible that we carry a negative obsession presence that has been attracted to the body part or area due to a repeating imbalance, pain and trauma.

When I was first introduced to these obsession presences, I was recovering from a serious concussion. It had been three years since I had had that concussion but some of my geographic orientation senses were not working well. I often felt out of balance in space, when leaning over, trying to perform certain yoga asanas or when I had to change direction very suddenly. In working with a hands-on-healer, she experienced a presence in my brain that when released resulted in the geographic orientation senses, vastly improving. The term for this presence was given as a negative obsession presence.

After this discovery, I checked my entire body for these presences and found them in every place where I had had trauma energy including in scars from cesarean operations, my knees, the bones of my spine, in my eyes, in the tissues of my buttocks and other areas as well. In working with clients, these negative obsession presences were frequently found in areas where there had been surgery or major trauma and where there were still sensations in the body from the original surgical or trauma experience.

They are not spirits, exactly. They are energy thought forms that manifest due to emotionally charged thoughts. They do keep the body from fully healing but they are not due to a person's spirit rather they are thought energy presences.

One of the characteristics of this type of energy is that this it resides in a very specific body area. An obsession presence's influence on the body is limited to the body part it has attached to or perhaps resides in. However, it is not uncommon to find between 8 and 12 of these negative obsession presences in one person's body especially if great pain, sorrow or trauma has been experienced. I have the energetic sense that these presences are small in scope and can easily be cast out with the identification of their presence in a body. They can also attach to an animal as well.

Further, it was revealed that these negative obsession presences can attach to our energetic bodies as well as to our physical bodies. These energetic bodies include, the emotional, mental, thermal and spiritual bodies. So, if you suspect you may have one of these negative obsession presences, it is a good idea to do a scan for these in your energy field and cast them out using the same protocol for casting out attached energy spirits given above. Substitute "negative obsession presence" whenever "negative spirit attachment" is used.

# CHAPTER ELEVEN

# Advanced Healing Interventions

YOU CAN GO DEEPER STILL. This chapter explores a range of topics related to advanced healing. The goal is to introduce these topics to begin to expand your thinking regarding the vast nature of healing options available to you with Divine Healing. If you are in need of using these advanced healing methods, the way forward will manifest in a meditative process or perhaps from an advanced spiritual healer when the timing is right to obtain this information. In the meantime, just knowing such healing options exist is mind expanding and directly affects our ability to set down our doubt and hesitations with regard to our perceived boundaries regarding Divine Healing.

## CLEARING FOR VOW CONTRACTS

The most challenging of situations are those that are chronic in nature and where seemingly, all possible remedies have already been tried. When this seems to be the case, and a person is still manifesting undesirable symptoms, you have to look further afield for other plausible situations that could be causing present day imbalances. This is exactly how this information regarding previously taken vows came to my awareness. Previous vows that have been taken in another incarnation, may still be binding for a person until that person releases him or herself from that vow energy. All vows taken have to be released in the environment in which they were originally taken.

One client I had known for several years reported that she had been suffering from tight finances for years. She felt she had tried everything to offer her services including creating a blog, newsletter, free consultations, and advertisements. All she had tried appeared to be to no avail. We began to speak about what might be the reasons behind not being able to have sufficient business to support her comfortably. We eventually came to the question as to whether or not she may have taken a vow of poverty in some previous life that was directly affecting her in the present moment.

In Sacred Silence, it was indicated that she had taken a vow of poverty and that energy was still present in her subconscious, unconscious and supra-conscious fields. When we cleared for this blocked energy along with all the other energies we had cleared over a few months all relating to poverty, she began to have new repeat clients. Her state of hand-to-mouth living, changed to a situation with sufficient and appropriate clients.

There are several types of vows that might have been readily taken in religious orders across the globe including; vow of celibacy, vow of chastity, vow of poverty, vow of fidelity, vow of duty, vow of self denial, vow of sacrifice, vow of suffering, and vow of obedience. Each of these vows would have been undertaken in earnest and then reinforced by the specific communities at the time.

If the energetic imprint of such vows remains in your energy field at the subconscious, unconscious level or supra-conscious level, this can lead to chronic imbalances in your current life. The lasting power you have given that vow while in this dimension, in body, will manifest in various imbalances especially to those seeking balance, peace, and unity with All That Is. All vows taken in this dimension need to be released consciously in this dimension to free you of that energy and the subsequent manifestations of the vow.

One client had been in two marriages in which she described herself as feeling trapped, unappreciated, and unable to easily fly free on her own. Though lots of healing work around anger and sadness had taken place, eventually it was revealed that my client did indeed carry the vow of sacrifice in her energetic field. Her entire life had consisted of working for others in the family without stopping to think about what she wanted and how she wanted it. Further, the magnitude of the self-sacrifice had to be huge in order for it to be worthy of her commitment to sacrifice her own well being for others. When this blocked energy cleared at both the unconscious and supra-conscious levels, she reported feeling deeply more peaceful and at ease in her own energy.

In order to be free of these types of vows and their impact on your life, you need to name the vows you are carrying and cast them out of your energy field at all levels of consciousness.

Speak aloud words in italics to give them more form and power in this dimension.

1.  *I open Sacred Space* (See the Six-Step Spiritual Healing Protocol or adapt as desired.)
2.  *I ask for guidance for the type of vow I have taken that is no longer serving me.*
3.  Select the type of vow taken from some of the following options; vow of celibacy, vow of chastity, vow of poverty, vow of fidelity, vow of duty, vow of self denial, vow of sacrifice, vow of obedience, vow of suffering, etc.
4.  *I call for the continuous clearing of all blocked energy including emotional, mental, thermal, spiritual, hereditary line, karmic, curse, and spell energies contributing to conscious, subconscious, unconscious, and supra-conscious vow of [name the vow] trauma energy and all symptoms.*
5.  *Clear all blocked energy back through all time and space, from the memories and patterns in my energetic field, from originating sources and down to the cellular memory level in the physical body. I call for my release from the vow of [name the vow] and for all manifestations of this vow of [name the vow] to rebalance.*
6.  *I call for the Divine Beings in this Sacred Healing and Wisdom circle to send all this healing out around the globe to thousands, or millions of others who may need this same healing today.*
7.  *I am deeply grateful for all the support and healing grace, and for the presence of specific Divine Beings who participated in the healing energy. Thank you and So It Is!*

## CLEARING FOR SOUL CONTRACTS

A soul contract is a contract made at the soul level at some time in the past that is affecting one's current lifetime. These contracts are more binding and perhaps more deeply buried in one's energy field than is a sacred vow. A contract is made before you enter into body and is a major theme for your life here on Earth.

Often a soul contract is made to make amends for past-perceived sins or poor life choices in other lifetimes. For example, one client was manifesting chronic depression and after months of clearing other trauma energies directly affecting depression, nothing seemed to be able to provide a lasting sense of peace and balance.

We began to work with a vow of self-punishment and even after that cleared energetically; there were still bouts of depression and hopelessness. We then began work on a soul contract of self-punishment taken as a result of thoughts that person had had about what was needed to make amends for perceived bad behavior and actions in a previous life.

Such soul contracts are often made in a lower state of consciousness than the current level of consciousness in this lifetime. When this is recognized, a soul contract can be rewritten or declared void. This releases the person from that previous contract or changes the contract to be more compatible with their current level of consciousness.

Until, for example, you realize that self-punishment is not needed for past errors, tough soul contracts can have very difficult consequences in a current lifetime. We are the ones who need to forgive ourselves. Divine Source has already forgiven us but we tend to carry un-forgiveness of self for lifetimes. If you have indeed done some heinous deed that you need to make amends for, you are not the one who needs to put that in place. Karma works perfectly well on its own, as it is a Universal Law that is self-regulating.

However, you create a soul contract therefore you can change it when you recognize that your life is being negatively run by such a soul contract.

Speak aloud words in italics to give them more form and power in this dimension.

1. *I open Sacred Space* (See Six-Step Spiritual Healing Protocol or adapt language as desired.)
2. *I ask for guidance for the type of soul contract I have taken that is no longer serving me well.*
3. Select one of the following types of soul contracts. Soul contract; of celibacy, of chastity, of poverty, of duty, of self-punishment, of fidelity, of self denial, of sacrifice, of obedience, of suffering, etc.

4. Select one of the following options appropriate for your situation. The first one is the cessation of an existing soul contract. The second one is an adjustment of an existing soul contract.

5. *I command that every aspect of this soul contract [name the soul contract] is no longer a part of my soul journey in this lifetime. It is completed. And so it is! Manifest immediately.*

6. *I command that my current soul contract of poverty (or of sacrifice, of suffering, etc.) be amended to a soul contract for the judicious use of abundant resource, (or of effective boundaries, of joyous living, etc.) And so it is! Manifest immediately.*

7. *I call for the Divine Beings in this Sacred Healing and Wisdom circle to send all this healing out around the globe to thousands, or millions of others who may need this same healing today*

8. Give thanks in any way that is appropriate for this healing work. Here is one example.

   *My deep appreciation for all the healing and guidance, that has led me to declare the completion of my soul contract (or to create a more appropriate soul contract, to adjust my former soul contract, etc.). I am both thrilled to be conscious enough to see what can be released in this lifetime and to be supported in doing this spiritually. I offer my sincere thanks for the Divine Beings working with me in this effort. And so it is! Amen*

## DIVINE ENERGY BATHS

So many individuals in body do not get enough sleep or a sufficient quality of sleep to renew their energy, endurance, and stamina so they can move through their days with grace and ease. Common responses to insufficient energy include drinking caffeinated drinks and overeating, especially sweets, trying to get enough energy to meet daily responsibilities. These habits have their own drawbacks over time and consuming these foods for energy usually has limited impact before the blood sugar either spikes or crashes or before we negatively affect our sleep due to too much caffeine.

Divine Soaks are great spiritual alternatives to the issue of tiredness, insufficient energy, and creating a negative spiral of poor food and drink options in the quest for more energy. Divine Soaks or Divine Light Baths are very underused sources of extra energy that have no bad side effects at all.

Speak all italicized words out loud. Lie down and close your eyes after opening Sacred Space. Call in the needed healing. Lying meditation is specifically for healing. Closing your eyes and focusing your mind on you own inner energy helps with the body's ability to receive the Divine Light Baths.

1. *I open this Sacred Healing and Wisdom Circle with my eternal energy and welcome into the space the Ascended Masters, the Cosmic Light Beings of the Universe, the Divas and Nature Intelligences, the Angelic Host and the Divine Healing Entities of Highest Light from all traditions.*

2. *I call for the most effective Divine healing vibrations from the Divine Healing Entities and any other appropriate sources available to me, to expand and support my energy resources to help me meet my responsibilities today with grace and ease.*

3. Remain lying down for a minimum of 8 minutes, knowing that you are receiving the supportive healing vibrations you need. Imagine Divine White and Golden Light entering your body from above you, below you, to the left and right of you, coming through your head, feet and hands.

4. *I give thanks for the healing energy I have received for my day. And So It Is!*

If you find your energy begins to flag later in the day, repeat this process. You can only receive the needed additional energy resources for the day. Each day this is needed, you have to ask for the resources for your day.

## TECHNIQUE TO ENHANCE PERSONAL ENERGY RESOURCES

There is another way to enhance your personal energy resources with the use of light energy. When you need to have more energy than your body has, you can use any small flashlight, headlamp, or small infrared penlight to raise the available energy resources you require.

I first learned of this technique from a physical therapist who had been taught to use an infrared pen light on the back of each knee for two minutes, every two hours when traveling, to reduce jet lag. This technique has revolutionized international travel for me as well as for many others.

Further, after I arrived at our destination, my travel companions and I would also take breaks when sightseeing to recharge our energy. While seated, we passed the infrared pen light down the line with each person using the pen light for two minutes behind the each knee, at the crease. You can hold the light right next to pant or leggings and that works just fine. We all felt our energy refreshed so that we could continue our day.

Since that time I have also had occasion to use both a small flashlight and a headlamp with LED lights to refresh and stimulate my body's energy so that I might concentrate more effectively or simply be able to function when a nap was not possible. When traveling across time zones, using a LED headlamp or small flashlight is an excellent way to arrive refreshed and able to function fully in the new time zone. When crossing time zones, it is necessary to use the light source behind each knee crease every two hours beginning at departure and ending with the last two-hour period near or after arrival at your destination.

## TALKING TO YOUR BODY

I was told about an amazing healing experience by a fellow meditator. She shared that Dr. Hew Len, a psychiatrist in Hawaii working in a mental institute for the criminally insane, began on his first day by looking at each patient's file picture and saying, " I am sorry, Please forgive me, I love you, Thank you". He did this everyday for each patient. In time, all these patients left the mental institute and resumed their lives. He never even saw these patients. [14]I was deeply touched by this story.

I began using these words when faced with serious pain and imbalance in my body. I had many occasions to use these words. I would hold my body area with my hands and repeat these healing words several times a day. I immediately felt a lessening of pain and it helped to remind myself that I was on the same team as my body. It helped me realize that my body was talking to me in the only way it could, through discomfort or pain. It helped me to really appreciate my body's efforts to communicate with me regarding the imbalance I was feeling.

With practice I began to empathize, appreciate, and cherish my knowing body. I learned that my body was desperately trying to speak to me. My body and I became a team. I began asking more deeply what I needed to understand from my body, and I would get insights of the core issues manifesting as the physical imbalances. I became more loving of my physical body. I healed age-old judgments regarding the seemingly constantly aching body and began to realize that in all the years of chronic pain, my body had relentlessly been trying to speak to me so I could heal.

## HEART HEALING – OBSERVATIONS FROM CASES

Physical heart imbalances are one of the most challenging areas where carrying one's own pain and other people's pain and sorrow manifests. In working with heart imbalances, in partnership with Divine Healing Entities, I have experienced all of the following healings through Divine vibrational interventions at the physical level for the healing of hearts. There has been healing for blocked arteries and veins including major and minor ones. There has been healing for every artery in the heart when looking in the aggregate at my clients. There have been healings for every chamber of the heart, for heart artery aneurisms, blood clots, and healings for all cardiac valves. There has been healing for the pericardium. There have been healings for every quadrant of the heart. I suspect that every part of the heart could be addressed through spiritual healing if needed.

Often the imbalances show up as a higher than normal blood pressure for a person but sometimes the symptoms have been mild to strong discomfort in the area of the heart, burning throat, stomach indigestion, and a pulling of tissue in the heart area to name a few. In almost all instances, there have been blocked energies of subconscious, unconscious and supra-conscious echo pain and empathic identification trauma energies contributing to the heart imbalances. (See Chapter Thirteen, Carrying Other People's Pain and Sorrow.)

When physical imbalances are indicated in the body, it is necessary to clear both unseen blocked energies and to call in Divine vibrational intervention healing for specific areas of the heart in the physical body.

Use the Six-Step Spiritual Healing Protocol for calling in healing for the specific areas of imbalance in your heart. Name the specific imbalance you are dealing with and call for the healing with language such as *left ventricle trauma energy and all symptoms* or *four blocked cardiac arteries trauma energy and all symptoms including high blood pressure*. At the same session, call for *Divine vibrational healing intervention from the Level 8 Himalayan Healing Entities and the Angels of the heart working together for continuous healing until such time as all physical imbalances are in Right Relationship with All That Is.*

When receiving any type of Divine healing support both the unseen energies as well as the physical body itself need to heal. Therefore, there are often restrictions on what you can do after divine surgery until the physical body is completely healed. Typically you need to rest one or two days and refrain from any physical exertion other than being around your home. There are frequently guidelines given with regard to the level of acceptable physical exertion, walking, yoga, yard work, etc. There is always a ban on lifting for 10 – 14 days especially with artery and valve healing.

In all cases I have worked with, when the healing has been called in, the heart has healed. This is simply beyond our understanding at the human level. We are so blessed, loved and cared for. We can call in the healing we need and receive it not only energetically but physically as well.

## BASIC HUMAN DESIRE TRAUMA

In The Art of Selflove, by Frank M. Lobsiger[15], there is a section he calls "four basic wants of the little-i." Lobsiger states that "there are four basic wants that the little-i is instinctively programmed to chase after in order to satisfy them." [16]

I think of the little-i as the small self, viewing the world outside of the eternal or True Self with human lenses. In my work, I find that this characterization of human wants and desires is completely true. Like any dimension of your human experience, these basic desires can be a natural part of life. Problems arise, however, when the basic desires or wants become a major or the only focus of your life. Every person I have worked with is being run by one or all of these four basic wants at the conscious, subconscious, unconscious or supra-conscious level. Lobsiger calls these four basic wants:

- The want to be/feel safe,
- The want to be/feel loved,
- The want to be/feel satisfied,
- The want to be/feel in control[17]

The challenge is to determine what repeating behaviors in our lives are connected with an overly dependent focus on these specific wants and desires such that they become the source of trauma in and of themselves. You can clear for the dominance of these wants or self-perceived needs from all levels of consciousness.

I worked with a client who was dealing with the traumatic death of a sibling, chronic anxiety, chronic sense of feeling overwhelmed, chronic inability to make decisions, a demanding need to capture stories in writing from his past and an inability to accomplish the present work he needed to do. When we went into Sacred Space and listened, he was carrying subconscious and unconscious desire to feel safe and subconscious and unconscious desire to feel in control. These energies were cast out of his energy field using the Healing Protocol. The energy during this clearing was physically expansive for him in that he felt the shifts literally being received in his body. As he was released from these trauma energies, peace was restored to his entire energy field.

To effectively do this work, the first step is to accurately describe the imbalanced energies that are reoccurring in your life. These are the behaviors, thoughts and feelings you know about and see. Then you look behind those for determination of which of these four basic wants of the small self could be fueling these frequent manifestations. Once overarching human wants are named, the human desire and all the manifestations of this desire can be cleared from one's energy field.

Another client came to me with chronic behavior manifesting as repeatedly losing her temper, lashing out at others when she was tired, feeling cranky and frustrated with her spouse, and stridently blaming others, even around small issues. She wanted to clear all these behaviors as they had been with her in some form or another for over 30 years. She felt they were totally at odds with the rest of her behaviors that were mostly peaceful, kind, and considerate. She reported feeling as if run by some unknown energy that repeatedly rendered her unable to respond to certain situations with grace and ease.

In Sacred Space, we found that she was carrying unconscious desire to feel in control. This blocked energy was causing all the manifestations she had identified. We used the Healing Protocol to clear the unconscious want to be/feel in control and all the specific ways it was manifesting in her behavior. After this clearing, she reported feeling freed, grateful, and at ease with knowing these old behaviors could finally be laid to rest because the motivating wants and feelings, had been cleared completely from her energy field. After the healing, she reported that none of the behaviors that had been manifesting were showing up in her life at all.

This set of four overarching desires and needs provides a great place to work with combinations of undesirable energy especially when it has been in your field for many years. Here are the steps you could use to do this.

Speak aloud words in italics to give them more form and power in this dimension.

## Protocol for Clearing Human Desire Trauma Energy

1. *I open Sacred Space (See the Six-Step Spiritual Healing Protocol or adapt language as desired.)*
2. *I ask for guidance about these four desires I may be carrying that may be negatively affecting my thoughts and actions. The desire to feel: safe, loved, satisfied, in control*
3. *I call for the continuous clearing of all blocked emotional, mental, thermal, spiritual, hereditary line, karmic, curse and spell energies from the following levels; conscious, subconscious, unconscious and supra-conscious contributing in any way to my desire to feel safe (or loved, satisfied, in control) trauma energy and all manifestations of these imbalances in my body and life.*
4. *I send out this healing energy across this planet to millions of others needing this healing energy received here today.*
5. *My profound thanks for the Divine Partners working with me and for all the guidance and healing given here today.*

## STRUCTURAL REBALANCING

Structural rebalancing is a powerful expansive method of Divine Healing that restructures one's body. It can also be used to restructure an organization, government, economic system, political system, racial injustice, religious history or educational system, etc. The training to be able to call this healing energy into this dimension required that I sit for months focusing on sacred geometric forms known in the Universe. I learned their names and was always searching for more and different types of sacred geometric forms.

Archangel Metatron oversaw and guided this training for me. This Archangel is often pictured holding the Metatron Cube above his head. The Metatron Cube is itself a form of sacred geometry. There are numerous designs that are considered sacred in their sense of balance. When I began this work, these designs were outside of my body and were things I was trying to take into myself, if you will. The guidance given during my training period was to look at these sacred geometric forms and then name them. Over many months, as the training completed, I was told that the forms had gone inside my being and were no longer outside of my energy field.

After that happened, I was able to work with structural rebalancing in many venues as guided by Divine Knowing. One experience working to rebalance the energy of a cathedral led me to sit inside a cathedral in Switzerland. My spiritual journey took me deep into the ground on which the cathedral stood. All the beauty, color, and splendor of the visible cathedral disappeared as we went deeper and deeper into the earth underneath the structure. At one point, there were simply grey blocks of concrete and then there was nothing left in the vision but the earth itself. I was guided to keep calling for structural rebalancing of the religious precepts affecting this Cathedral.

The process seemed to go to the middle of the Earth and all form of the building disappeared while the work was going on. When the structural rebalancing was complete, I was released from the depths of the earth and slowly came back ascending to the surface, to the present day energy of the Cathedral. I was led to understand there had been a deep cleansing of the history and structure of the entire basis of the cathedral history, the religious precepts it was based upon, and the form of the building itself from the deep past.

I did not receive a detailed account of what had happened. I simply knew that my job was complete and if more clarity was needed, that would be given. Following these types of experiences, I was eventually led to work with individuals who had experienced some traumatic form of abuse or health trauma in their present or distant past. The detox from this type of healing is significant and therefore you need to be very sure as a healer, that the timing is appropriate before undertaking this work with others.

## DARK NIGHT OF THE SOUL

At one point in my practice, I found myself totally stumped with regard to five different clients who were not continuing to heal. Each one was working with a different set of imbalances from depression to insomnia with another experiencing unexplained exhaustion and two others with chronic sciatica and bipolar disorder. I was at a loss to help any of them beyond the place they found themselves to be. My response was to ask for help in Sacred Space. I asked for specific guidance as to how I might continue to be supportive of these clients and their health.

I was referred to the concept of the Dark Night of the Soul. I had heard of this term and read of different Saint's experiences that they had termed their Dark Night of the Soul. Generally, a Dark Night of the Soul is a journey you are on, often unbeknownst to you, in order to become free of a series of blocked energies manifesting as imbalances in your life.

I had experienced two Dark Night of the Soul journeys in my own life. One was with my oldest son who was sick and out of balance for over two years when he was a child. The other was with my own back pain for 19 years. I had a basic understanding of what these journeys could entail and could bring about in terms of deep healing and rebalancing.

A Dark Night of the Soul, as I currently think of it, is a spiritual journey that can have multiple imbalances and challenges - emotional, mental, physical, spiritual - that return repeatedly until there is spiritual help and guidance sought and received. It is a spiritual journey that can last weeks or months or years.

One question I had to address with each of these five clients was if structural rebalancing was needed or not. That would have been my first choice with the known level of presenting complexities. However, in each of these client cases, structural rebalancing was not compatible. This had been part of my frustration as well, as it had seemed I was out of options.

In response to my question to Divine Source, I was instructed to work with each person as if they were in a Dark Night of the Soul journey. So framed, their progress along this journey could be mapped as to the percentage of their completion of this journey. Each journey would have a beginning point and an end point and places along the journey that could be checked for progress.

In each session, I was instructed to clear for blocked energies manifesting as a Dark Night of the Soul with regard to a specific disorder such as bipolar disorder or chronic insomnia, depending on the specific individual. The nature of the Dark Night of the Soul needed to be specified with regard to the overall purpose. In at least two cases, individuals were actually on two different Dark Night of the Soul journeys, at the same time. I would use specific terms such as "Dark Night of the Soul for Jim with regard to his heart imbalances and all symptoms", for example.

The most helpful part of this approach to healing was that after each clearing of the indicated blocked energies from specific levels of consciousness, I could then ask what percentage of the Soul's journey was complete. This was a new idea to me with regard to working with complex sets of imbalances. Parts of this approach to "mapping progress", I had certainly worked with before but not with this level of complexity.

I had previously worked with Divine Source to request the level of efficiency of a specific organ as well as for systems like the immune system or the visual or hearing system. I would request the efficiency of the visual system and we might start at 58% efficiency. We would continue healing until we were getting 97% efficiency or higher.

This was very helpful to my clients and to me because though overall healing progress was being made, no visible indication could be seen on the physical level. With some of these processes taking weeks or months, it was very helpful to be able to chart progress, however slowly that was happening.

Adapting these techniques to a Dark Night of the Soul journey led to widely differing blocked energies, often seemingly unrelated to our overall focus of the healing. For example, in an energy clearing session, we might jump from depression imbalances to childhood abuse, to a specific relationship, and onto a soul contract. Each step would be indicated By Divine Knowing, along the Dark Night of the Soul journey regarding a specific imbalance such as ALS, chronic venereal disease, or chronic loss of hearing.

When I worked with one client on a Dark Night of the Soul journey, regarding her mental health, Divine Knowing included all related symptoms pertinent to the journey as well the central focus of the journey. As we began, neither my client nor I knew that her dark dreams were directly related to her overall soul journey regarding her mental health. We discovered that as her known mental health issues were identified and healed, her years of dark dreams disappeared as well. We were totally unaware that these imbalances were directly related.

As more experiences were given, there were at least three times when the entire Dark Night of the Soul clearing, addressing ongoing issues for years, was completed in a one-hour session. Of course, this needed to be followed by a period of healing for the body and attention to all remaining symptoms but the underlying blocked issues were all addressed in an hour session.

Our physically dense bodies are the last place healing fully manifests. We can determine healing is happening in the spiritual, mental, or emotional bodies long before the physical body fully receives the healing energies and manifests balance. Thus, using a mapping process like Dark Night of the Soul journey has been most helpful in determining where you are along the continuum with a specific healing approach. The Dark Night of the Soul approach to healing for complex issues is an extraordinarily powerful approach, beyond measure, especially with chronic conditions.

This process of using the Dark Night of the Soul journey with regard to a specific set of imbalances was an amazingly effective adaptation for healing chronic issues with seemingly unrelated causes and symptoms. This new approach enabled clear direction to be given in Sacred Space about the entire set of underlying issues affecting an overall chronic imbalance.

In doing this work, I often felt as if I was on a guide leash, albeit one with great wisdom and compassion, being led to blocked energies I would have never associated with the stated goal. The Divine Partnership in which I work has been continually supportive, instructional, and constantly responsive. This help and support is available to all who may seek such connection with Divine Source.

# CHAPTER TWELVE

# Deconstructing Imbalances

HOW DO YOU PUT IT ALL TOGETHER? In the four previous chapters, I have described in some detail a range of methods to call forth healing for particular kinds of imbalances and blocked energies with various techniques and methods. Over the years, I have developed a sense of when to use what kind of approach for which problems. Over time, you will learn this as well.

Some imbalances will be healed when using the Six-Step Spiritual Healing Protocol in Chapter Seven, but many will need further work. We spend a lifetime accumulating blocks and imbalances and it may take a long time to clear them fully. Also, many of us often enter into this lifetime carrying unhealed energies of the past. Many issues are chronic and will need a full range of healing interventions to heal.

Therefore, in this chapter I have provided the general order in which I tend to apply different healing modalities to situations that require more than one approach. I have numbered them for convenient reference.

Remember that when using any of these approaches, you should begin with the first three steps of the Six-Step Spiritual Healing Protocol. The major reason you always work within a Sacred Healing and Wisdom Circle and then Prepare and Listen is that you are seeking guidance as to how to effectively use the vast range of healing modalities and determine the true name of the imbalance. You want to be working in partnership with Divine Beings of Highest Light to be most effective. The second major reason to open and work in Sacred Space is that you will eliminate all possibility of a negative spirit entering into your work.

Working in partnership with Spirit increases the probability that the combined wisdom will result in expansive knowing beyond your own. If you don't work in partnership with Divine knowing, you may well find it difficult to know what healing modalities to call forth.

When you work in partnership with Divine Beings, your combined efforts produce the best results in an easily accessible process. The combined efforts of your partnership brings forth healing for all situations, though perhaps not always as you might expect it to happen.

The Six-Step Spiritual Healing Protocol is by definition "basic." You may need to deconstruct the imbalance you are working with and apply other modalities or the same modalities more deeply. After you have opened Sacred Space, Prepared and Listened, and Named the Imbalance, use the process described in the following pages to work through the additional modalities that have been explained in detail in the previous four chapters.

This entire process may take days, months or years. This is an eternal process for all time, in all forms or in formlessness, wherever you may find yourself or another with whom you are called to work. The process can continue until such time as all blocked energies have been identified and cleared so that the imbalances being addressed can come into Right Relationship with All That Is.

## 1. CLEAR IMBALANCES AND CALL FORTH HEALING

Clear continuously all blocked emotional, mental, thermal, spiritual, hereditary line, karmic, curse and spell energies at the conscious, subconscious, unconscious, and supra-conscious levels manifesting as (the imbalance) and all symptoms. See the Six-Step Spiritual Healing Protocol for the full explanation.

Call for the most appropriate Himalayan (or Casa, Bhutan, Canadian, etc.) Healing Entities working with the Angels of (the imbalance) to manifest Divine vibrational intervention healing for (the imbalance) at the highest possible rate of healing.

## 2. CALL FOR STELLAR HEALING ENERGY

If consistent healing is not manifesting perhaps there is a specific type of healing energy needed that has yet to be called in. Divine Stellar Healing Energy, as shared earlier, is the energy of the moon, sun, and stars. We are made of the same chemical building blocks as these celestial bodies. Therefore, Divine Stellar Healing Energy is another source of healing vibration that can greatly benefit our bodies and energy fields.

Call forth Divine Stellar Healing Energy for (the imbalance) trauma energy and all symptoms. See Chapter Eight, Divine Stellar Healing Energy, for more details.

### Choice point

The order in which you use the next four healing modalities depends on the nature of the imbalance. If the imbalance is physical such as: the respiratory system, an infection, or a chronic disease in the body, just continue through the modalities as far as needed in numbered order.

If, however, the imbalance is emotional, mental or spiritual such as: exacerbated fear, hopelessness, doubt of Divine love, or self-worth trauma energy; go next to modality 5 - Negative Spirit Attachments, and 6 - Negative Obsession Presence. Then, if more healing is needed, return to 3 - Gene-Induced Trauma Energy and 4 - Gestational Trauma Energy and then continue through the remaining steps, 7, 8, 9, and 10. The link between emotional, mental, and spiritual imbalances and negative spirit attachments and obsession presences is so common that I recommend you work through these modalities in this order for highest impact.

### 3. CLEAR FOR GENE-INDUCED TRAUMA ENERGY

To determine if gene-induced trauma energy is a factor in the imbalance you are addressing, begin by declaring, *"I am (or, name of person is) manifesting gene-induced (the imbalance) trauma energy"*. Get a confirmation of this either through use of a pendulum or through silent discernment. If possible, determine the number of genes involved. If a specific number of involved genes is not available, clear for *"all the genes affecting the imbalance"*.

Call for the rebalancing of (specific number of genes or all genes) involved in (the imbalance) trauma energy and all symptoms.

Call for the most appropriate Himalayan (or Casa, Bhutan, Canadian, etc.) Healing Entities and Angels to rebalance all genes contributing to gene-induced (the imbalance) trauma energy and all symptoms at the highest possible rate of healing.

Clear repeatedly until no further genes are indicated for this imbalance. See Chapter Nine, Gene-Induced Imbalances for more details.

## 4. CLEAR FOR GESTATIONAL TRAUMA ENERGY

Gestational trauma energy refers to the time in utero and all occurrences during that time that are still present in one's system. To determine if gestational trauma energy regarding the imbalance in question requires healing, you need to begin by declaring, *"I am (or name person is) manifesting gestational trauma energy affecting (the imbalance) trauma energy and all symptoms."*

Determine via a pendulum or through silent discernment if gestational trauma energy is present for you or the person in question. If yes, clear first for the blocked energy at the unseen levels, followed by calling in Divine vibrational healing for the imbalance itself as indicated below.

*I call for continuous clearing of all blocked emotional through spell energies and everything in between at the conscious, subconscious, unconscious, and supra-conscious levels manifesting as gestational (the imbalance) trauma energy and all symptoms.*

*I call forth continuous Divine vibrational intervention healing from the most appropriate levels of the Himalayan (or Casa, Bhutan) Healing Entities and Angels to rebalance all (the imbalance) trauma energy and all symptoms.* See Chapter Eight, Healing Entity Groups for additional details.

## 5. CLEAR FOR NEGATIVE SPIRIT ATTACHMENTS

There are three types of negative spirit attachments and one type of unattached spirit. When working with anyone who experiences a sudden observable jump in negative energies, there may be a negative spirit attachment involved. Extreme emotions, sudden malaise, the inability to be calm or sleep, or great fear can indicate a negative spirit attachment. As explained earlier in Chapter Ten, all spirits of any kind either attached or unattached belong in Divine Light and not in this dimension.

It is common for newly passed individuals to remain a few days after their death as they prepare to leave this dimension. They may be saying goodbye to loved ones or waiting until there is a memorial service for them before leaving for the Light. This is normal and after all such public gatherings for this person are complete, their place is towards the Light in Divine Eternal Space. This is true for all spirits of any type. They cause imbalances for themselves and others by staying in this dimension out of form.

Therefore, it is important to know how to work with these spirits when they are present for you or for another person with whom you are working. Refer to Chapter Ten for the complete process for clearing these negative attached and unattached spirits. Here is a summary of the steps and order to follow taken from the more detailed explanation in Chapter Ten.

Determine if there is a negative spirit attachment and its type (attached, obsession attachment, possession attachment) or if there is an unattached spirit. Negative attached spirits are actually attached to a person's energetic field or to their physical field or both. The unattached spirits are in a person's vicinity. Both types can be disruptive to a person's energy.

Clear all blocked energies at all levels of consciousness that have attracted the specific type of negative spirit to you or to another person.

Command the negative spirit to the Light. See Chapter Ten for detailed steps.

## 6. CLEAR FOR NEGATIVE OBSESSION PRESENCE

A negative obsession presence can reside in any part of the body or a person's energy field thereby hampering healing. This is a lesser order of magnitude than negative spirits attached to a person. This negative obsession presence is more akin to a thought presence in a specific body part. Nonetheless, such negative obsession presences do directly impact healing. Here is a summary of needed steps to cast these presences out of one's body or energy field.

Clear all blocked emotional through spell energies and everything in between, at the conscious, subconscious, unconscious, and supra-conscious levels that have attracted a negative obsession presence to you or to another person.

Substitute "negative obsession presence" and the specific body part or system when casting out a presence of this kind. See Chapter Ten, Negative Obsession Presences for specific steps.

## 7. CLEAR FOR VOWS AND SOUL CONTRACTS

Check to see if you or the person you are working with carries either vow or soul contract trauma energies or both. These can impact your ability to heal. A sacred vow can have been made in another lifetime and still be affecting a person's ability to heal in this lifetime. A soul contract can be even more far reaching in its impact.

If you came into this world with a soul contract of self-punishment to make amends for deeds you deemed unacceptable, this can affect your health, your prosperity, your relationships or all three. Vows or contracts usually remain hidden until chronic life patterns manifest, requiring a deeper look into possible explanations. Imbalanced conditions in your life are often due to some type of imbalance at the unseen level. These topics are well worth exploring if such chronic conditions exist in your life. See Chapter Eleven, Clearing Vow Contracts and Clearing Soul Contracts.

## 8. CLEAR FOR BASIC HUMAN DESIRE TRAUMAS

At this point, if healing is still needed due to persistent, imbalances, clearing for basic human desire trauma energies can relieve wide reaching imbalances that touch on many aspects of your life or another's. If you, for example, are constantly seeking new friends, new places to visit, and other venues for proving yourself, you may be carrying desire to feel satisfied trauma energy. Until that desire or want energy is cleared, that inner sense of needing to constantly seek new venues will persist. See Chapter Eleven, Basic Human Desire Trauma for details.

## 9. INITIATE DARK NIGHT OF THE SOUL JOURNEY PROCESS

This process for healing is useful when a number of issues present themselves but it is unclear how they relate to each other. Issues with multiple sources and symptoms could be successfully addressed by using this process. Abuse, depression, inability to keep a job, and chronic insomnia trauma energies would be examples of types of imbalances that might benefit from this process. When this process is initiated, it allows the person to see where they are along the journey which can be determined in Sacred Space. See Chapter Eleven, Dark Night of the Soul for specific guidance.

## 10. INITIATE STRUCTURAL REBALANCING

This process is useful when total rebalancing at the cellular level or foundational levels is needed. As explained earlier, structural rebalancing is calling forth the energy of sacred geometry for the healing of physical substances that make up any system, building, organization or part of the body. It is also helpful for imbalances in relationships, companies, governments, social issues, etc. See Chapter Eleven, Structural Rebalancing for additional details.

# CHAPTER THIRTEEN

# Calling Forth Healing for Others

IF YOU HAVE COME TO A PLACE in your spiritual journey where you feel called to work with others, this chapter gives effective ways to do that. One of the first questions often asked is how can I call in healing for others who themselves are not open to spiritual healing and prayer. At some levels of consciousness, people assume that if a person is not consciously open to healing at the conscious level, nothing can be done. This is not the case as we are all Divine Beings and calling in healing for others can often be received at the eternal soul level by a person even when they are consciously closed to spiritual healing at the physical level. This type of work though has some unique characteristics addressed in this chapter.

This chapter also addresses potential challenges when working with others regarding the taking on others' pain and sorrow and identifying with their pain and sorrow both of which can affect your own health and wellbeing.

## WORKING WITH THOSE CLOSED TO SPIRITUAL HEALING

There are those you may interact with, who are suffering from traumas of all kinds who themselves are closed to spiritual healing at the conscious level. I often get asked, "How can I work with loved ones who are not open to spiritual healing and prayer?"

If you have been doing spiritual healing for yourself for at least a year regularly, you are probably ready to call in healing for others whether or not they are open at the conscious level. When working with those closed to this type of healing, any healing you call forth is not likely to be recognized as help from you, even if you see or hear they are doing better.

So, if you choose this path to help others, you have to be content with the fact that you will get no credit or thanks for this work. You are not likely to be able to say after the fact, "well, I have been calling in this healing for you for the past three months," for example. This is because if a person is closed consciously to spiritual healing, they are most likely to see this as interference in their lives, stepping over the boundaries, and invading their space, even if they get better.

Those not open to spiritual healing frequently see themselves as completely separate from you and Divine Source. Therefore, unless they ask you or give you permission to help them by calling in healing energy, your actions will most likely be seen as "messing in their business." Whatever their issues are, they may well assume they are the only ones being affected by what they are going through or that at least the issue is private to them. This is sometimes the case even with close family members living in the same house. In summary, if a person has not asked you to help in this way, then you keep your own counsel and speak to no human being about what you are doing.

If you choose to call in healing for another person who is not consciously open to spiritual healing, you have to check to see if this work is yours to do. You must receive Divine confirmation that you are called to work in this way with the person in question. Then, you need to clear for blocked energy to spiritual healing before proceeding or they will not be able to receive the healing you are calling for them.

## Protocol For Those Closed to Spiritual Healing

State all steps out loud as indicated by italics.

1. *I open Sacred Space* (See Six-Step Spiritual Healing Protocol. Open the space with both your and the other person's human and eternal energies present in the Sacred Healing and Wisdom Circle.)
2. *Please confirm that this is my work to do with (name the person) and that I should proceed.* If confirmed proceed. If not confirmed or unclear, do not proceed.
3. *Sacred Flame within [name the person being supported], come forth. Clear continuously all emotional, mental, thermal, spiritual, hereditary line, karmic, curse and spell blocked energies at the conscious, subconscious, unconscious and supra–conscious levels*

*manifesting as spiritual healing trauma energy and all symptoms including being closed to spiritual healing.*

4. *Clear all blocked energies from originating lifetimes and sources, back through all time and space, from the cellular memory level in the physical body, from all memories and patterns in the energetic field manifesting as spiritual healing trauma energy and all symptoms.*

5. Repeat this healing now at the physical level as indicated in step 6. You need to be sure all is totally cleared from both the person's spiritual and physical energy fields.

6. *Sacred Flame within [name the person being supported], come forth. Clear continuously all emotional through spell energies and everything in between from the conscious, subconscious, unconscious and supra-conscious levels manifesting at the physical level as spiritual healing trauma energy and all symptoms including being closed to spiritual healing.*

7. *I give thanks for the Divine Partnership working with us today. And So It Is!*

This protocol enables the person you are concerned about to receive Divine Spiritual Healing. You then proceed to use the Six-Step Spiritual Healing Protocol to identify and clear the specific imbalances you are concerned about and call forth the clearing needed.

## WORKING WITH DIVINE BEINGS ON BEHALF OF ANOTHER

If you have misgivings or hesitations in using the above protocol, there are still ways to call forth healing energy for others. Even though you may not feel you understand the situation enough for you to call healing in for another yourself, there are options. Perhaps you simply want to use a more simplified approach to prayer and healing for others. I recommend the following approach to fit these conditions. This approach is also very effective when individuals are closed to each other and there are unresolved issues between the two individuals.

Rather than calling in the specific healing energy yourself using the Six-Step Spiritual Healing Protocol, you can send your call to those Divine Beings walking through life with the person or persons you are concerned about. This is represented in the triangle graphic below.

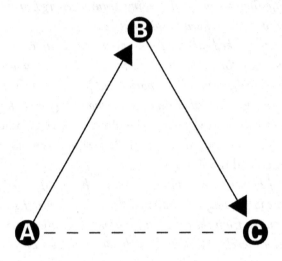

You are A. The group of Divine Beings is B. The person receiving the healing is C. The Divine Beings are walking with the person in question (C) during this lifetime.

You (A) are observing imbalances and their consequences for the person you are concerned about (C). Rather than raising these concerns directly with the person (C) for any number of reasons, you raise those issues with the Divine Beings (B) on behalf of person (C) in question.

With this approach, you still need to make sure that this person is open to Divine Healing before you ask for the specific help you think is needed from The Divine Beings. Follow the Protocol for Those Closed to Spiritual Healing above, if you suspect the person you are asking about is not open to Spiritual Healing. When that is called forth, the shift within the person being supported is instantaneous. Therefore you can continue immediately with the following Protocol to work with the Divine Beings who can direct healing to the desired person.

State all steps out loud as indicated by italics.

1. *I open this Sacred Healing and Wisdom circle with the Angelic Host, Ascended Masters, Cosmic Light Beings of the Universe, Devas and Nature Intelligences and Divine Healing Entities of Highest Light*

*from all traditions to work with [name the person]. I include both of our physical and Eternal Energies in this Circle.*

2. *I call forth the wisdom, knowledge and insight from the Divine Beings walking in this life with [name the person] for the healing of all blocked energies contributing to his/her addiction to drugs and alcohol (or depression, anger, loss of limb, etc.) trauma energy and all the symptoms including stealing (or feeling of instability, apathy, self-medicating in daily life, etc.).*

3. *Clear continuously all emotional, mental, thermal, spiritual, hereditary line, karmic, curse and spell blocked energies at the conscious, subconscious, unconscious and supra–conscious levels manifesting as addiction to drugs and alcohol (or name of imbalance) trauma energy and all symptoms, known and unknown.*

4. *We call forth the most appropriate Divine Healing Entities and Angels to work with [name the person] for Divine vibrational intervention healing at the physical level for full rebalancing and healing.*

5. *Thank you for your knowledge, power and healing assistance in this work with [name of person]. We are so blessed. And So It Is!*

## CARRYING OTHER PEOPLE'S PAIN AND SORROW

Many, if not all professionals working in helping fields with others have been trained not take on other people's pain. This is central to remaining healthy and whole when working with others in pain or in stress. If therapists or healers are not totally conscious of remaining free of others' pain and sorrow, they can end up with patients or client issues stuck in their own bodies as some form of imbalance. Generally, professional training is given during required courses for licensing to enable you to be conscious of when you are taking on other people's issues, pain, and sorrow.

If you are drawn to work with other people's imbalances in this lifetime, you are most likely to have done this in other forms before this lifetime. Therefore, you need to proactively pursue healing for what is likely to reside in your subconscious, unconscious, and supra-conscious fields with regard to others' pain and sorrow. It is very likely, that if you do not proactively seek this out, eventually the accumulation of this in your energetic and physical bodies will speak quite loudly to you.

Areas of needed healing can be indicated by physical, emotional, mental, or spiritual conditions that do not seem to come into balance. They can be indicated by a sense of feeling stuck, unmotivated, overwhelmed, dissatisfied. There is a good chance that you are carrying other people's pain or sorrow, whether consciously or not, if your work concerns: leading others, healing, counseling, working with patients, listening to plaintiffs, running a medical practice, caring for others, being a mediator, acting as an ombudsman, dealing with patterns of trauma of any kind. Most often the blocked energies are at the subconscious, unconscious or supra-conscious levels. The accumulation of this type of unconscious pain and sorrow over years can be devastating to your own health, in body, in mind or in spirit.

This past year I was been dealing with debilitating relentless pain in my left heal. The only exercise I could continue to do for several months was yoga. Eventually I was also able to ride a stationary bike. I tried everything I could think of to diminish the pain in my left heel and researched all the possible issues such a bone spurs, pulled ligaments, Achilles tendon, etc. I asked countless times in Sacred Space if I should seek medical help from a physician and repeatedly got "no". I even tried for a while to ignore this pain but hobbling around with increasing pain eventually needed some seriously dedicated attention. This attention time eventually coincided with a vacation where I was completely un-programmed.

I had lived with nineteen years of chronic back pain, as shared earlier. I therefore had lots of experience with my body speaking to me and me not understanding the messages. This experience felt completely as if I was missing the messages being given, though other healing was taking place along the way, the heel pain persisted.

I was fortunate to be able to ask another to help me determine what I was not able to hear. It was as if my foot was loudly screaming at me and I could not understand the meaning behind the language being used. After asking for help from another spiritual person, I got the insight and language to understand that I was carrying "echo pain" trauma energy and "empathic identification" trauma energy. Trauma energy as noted earlier is whole spectrum energy that covers all aspects of what is being identified.

In my case, both areas identified resided in my subconscious, unconscious field and supra-conscious levels. I could not even begin to imagine that I carried such blocked energies because I had never taken on other people's pain consciously in all the years I had worked with others.

I received these definitions through Divine Source while in meditation. "Echo pain trauma is other people's pain and sorrow. Empathic identification trauma energy is the process of deeply identifying with other people's traumas, health issues, relationship, losses, fears, etc. These are related in manifestation, but are dissimilar in vibration."

This means that these trauma energies are connected in how they manifest in our lives but they need to be addressed individually. In both of these types of trauma energy, the physical body and energy field can be affected. In my situation, these imbalances manifested physically due to my having a long history of learning to seek through the experience of body pain.

Since this time, I have worked with others who have been brought to this understanding of carrying others' pain and sorrow because their sleep has suffered, their emotions have bottomed out, their hearts were damaged, or their sense of being connected with Divine Source had been affected. All of these manifestations were indications of unseen echo trauma pain and unseen empathic identification trauma pain.

In my own experience, because I work not only with individuals but also at the global level, this pain and sorrow load was crippling me. After doing this healing for echo pain and empathic identification trauma energy almost every day for four months, I was finally free of both echo trauma pain and empathic identification energy.

My heel completely healed. In the worse times, I used all sorts of healing rubs, essential oils and ibuprofen to help alleviate the pain. I had been walking in "Crocs" for over five months before I received guidance as to what might be causing the pain. Slowly my other favorite shoes began manifesting as new options for me to wear.

Healing of this level of magnitude was life changing. I have never in all my years, felt this free and unburdened. When I shared this with those studying with me, their first question was how do we avoid this in our lives even after we clear it from our fields and are free of the blocked trauma energy in the present.

One way to address this is to open Sacred Space and set an eternal intention for this lifetime and all lifetimes to never take on and carry other people's trauma pain or to empathically identify with that pain and sorrow, consciously, subconsciously, unconsciously or supra-consciously in any work we do. Obviously, there are times when considering all eternity that we could be in devastating circumstances such as war, occupation, physical disaster, devastation or cruelty that deeply troubles our souls. However, this intention will stand for all time and would even in those situations, mitigate the severity of our reactions.

Pain and sorrow of others is not ours to take on. Indeed, even calling pain and sorrow to ourselves as a means of atonement or self-punishment is not in Right Relationship with All That Is. Setting such intentions or soul contracts for ourselves, in the larger sense, means that we have not forgiven ourselves wholly for what has occurred in the past.

I worked with a client who had taken vows of suffering thinking that this would be positive and cleansing for him. He had indeed had deep suffering in this lifetime. We were led to clear for his vow of suffering he had made in lifetime and at another level of consciousness that was no longer serving him.

Another major reason for not taking on another's pain is that is it their pain and sorrow to heal and learn from. Your taking on the pain of another is completely useless. It may even serve to prolong another's time for learning and for clearing their own pain through their own sources. You may still be tempted to try and alleviate another's pain and sorrow by taking it on, but besides the fact that you cannot do this effectively, it doesn't help. This is sometimes a misunderstanding of compassion for those who work to help others.

What does help is **non-attached compassion**. It is most helpful to offer love, compassion, and support but without becoming attached to another's path, issues, emotions, or their decisions. This way you can support others moving through their lives but without weighing yourself down with pain and sorrow that is not yours. It is worth noting that you cannot effectively help others if you are carrying the same unbalanced issues as they are. You will most often be emotionally or personally pricked by their journey because you need to do the same work as they need to do.

We are each Divine Beings at our core, so we are not without inner direction. No one is without this inner direction but many of us cannot readily access the meaning of repeating challenges and issues in our lives.

You may be able to listen, encourage, support, and witness along with others but once you cross the line to taking on their pain, you suffer right along with them and in the end taking on that suffering is not helpful to your own journey or theirs.

There are a few very specific exceptions with those who have already ascended to the Light and have returned to serve others here. There is a state of being where Ascended Beings can with their death take huge amounts of darkness, rage, imbalance and heartache with them into the Light for transformation. This is a special calling, outside of what we are speaking about here.

## CLEARING OTHERS' PAIN FROM YOUR ENERGY FIELD

When you begin to clear for echo trauma pain and empathic identification trauma energy, clear these processes separately. Preferably clear these imbalances on different days, to insure you are not overwhelmed with detox. All imbalances clearing from the conscious level will create detox in the physical body. This detox could be severe in the beginning and will lessen as you clear more and more. Tiredness and bowel changes are the most common detox symptoms. Other symptoms can include nausea, headaches, thirst, poor appetite, and poor sleep. A good rule of thumb is to take a break from clearing until detox symptoms are clear in the body, and then continue the healing process.

When no more detox at all is being felt, you can move to clear for both types of imbalances together, on the same day, at the same time.

*Protocol for clearing other's pain from your energy field*

1. *Open Sacred Space (see Six-Step Spiritual Healing Protocol)*
2. *I call forth the Sacred Flame within me to consume continuously all emotional through spell energies and all those in between from the conscious, subconscious, unconscious and supra-conscious levels manifesting as echo pain, (or empathic identification) trauma energy and all symptoms.*
3. *Consume all blocked energies from all time and space, from originating lifetime and sources, down to the cellular memory level, and from all memories and patterns in the energetic field. I call forth the highest rate of healing possible for this healing.*

4. *I call for all these energies to be transformed by Divine Light from blocked, stagnant, draining energies to balanced, flowing, and life affirming energy. And so it is!*
5. *We send out all of this healing around the globe for millions of others needing this healing today.*
6. *My profound thanks to all Divine Beings holding this Sacred Space with me in partnership to support this healing today.*

Repeat this process the next day for empathic identification trauma energy and all symptoms. Repeat, alternating between clearing for echo trauma pain and empathetic identification each day unless detox is still present from the previous healing. In that case, wait until all detox is clear to begin the process again. When your energy field remains stable, you can clear for both imbalances at the same time, on the same day.

Proceed with this work until you get confirmation that both types of these energies are completely gone from your conscious, subconscious, unconscious, and supra-conscious energy fields at both the spiritual and physical levels.

As a gross measure of the time this work takes, it has taken 100 days of daily work to completely clear all subconscious, unconscious, and supra-conscious echo pain and empathic identification trauma energy from my field. I did not begin with any conscious blocked energies of echo pain or empathic identification so we are speaking of major clearing work to be completely free of these influences. However with the call for the highest rate of healing to occur, you may be able to shorten the needed healing time.

Even when all the core energies have cleared, there may remain symptoms in the physical body that may continue to need clearing work. For example, Divine vibrational intervention healing may be needed for support of any physical imbalances such as an elbow, neck or other body part still manifesting imbalance. Refer to Divine Vibrational Intervention in Chapter 8 for instructions of how to proceed. Healing in the physical body is the last place for the full balance to manifest due to body density.

# CHAPTER FOURTEEN

# Global Healing

All healing for the Earth and its people has to be called in by humans in body. No one else can make this call for humans in this dimension. This is because each of us, at our core, is Divine and we each have free will. Our unhealed imbalances are why we are here in body, unless we have already ascended and have returned to serve others.

At some time you took on views, feelings, thoughts, and fears from an incomplete state of being related to your humanity and your Divinity. You have free will so you are the one who needs to call in the healing you want to see, the rebalancing you need, and the guidance you need. You are human in this dimension for a short while but your core is Divine and as such you have free will. No one other than you can determine your path, your desires, and your experiences.

God/Divine Source is a pure energy form of Wholeness, Balance, and Love. This energy form is constant in perfection and also expanding all the time through all the forms that have been made in the Image of God/ All That Is. God is not an entity looking on and saying, "Yes, send healing there or no, not yet". That concept found in the Old Testament of the Bible may have been a useful metaphor but it is inaccurate energetically.

Divine Source Energy is constant and at the same time ever expanding that constancy through your knowing and burgeoning awareness. This may seem to be a contradiction. It is not. As you, who are Divine Beings at your core, begin to operate from pure love and forgiveness. That is one way the God Energy expands.

The Oneness/God is not affected by pain, requests, trauma, loss, sorrow, guilt, beseeching, etc. The ability to receive Divine Source help may well be affected by imbalances but Divine Source remains constant.

We are the ones who have the responsibility and authority to call in Wholeness and Healing for self and others in this dimension. No one else can do this. God is perfect love, unchanging, totally constant, fully trustworthy. We are the ones changing as we become more aware of our eternal connection to Spirit.

You must commune with the Spirit of All That Is to learn that you are irrevocably connected for all eternity, with the Divine Whole/the Oneness/All That Is. As this happens for you, you learn how to bring that knowing to your own life. All too frequently many humans hold to a simplified version of "go to your Father and request all that is needed." This may eventually bring about energy changes, especially if you are asking with a deep hunger for healing for self and others. However, this is not generally the most effective way of bringing forth healing.

When you ask for healing in this way, you are seeing yourself as separate from Divine Source/God. This weakens your prayers because this characterization is energetically inaccurate. You are One with All That Is no matter what your life circumstances look like in this lifetime. Essentially, you are in consecutive earth settings, learning that you are part of the Great I AM Energy of All That Is. You come here over and over again, until you are completely free of ego energy running you. Then you can fully embrace your Oneness with All That Is, with God. Thus your prayers held in any other state than this are less than fully effective.

Nothing in this dimension is real or lasting except the energies of Love. Everything in this dimension decays and dies including your body. The only lasting energy is your Eternal Soul and All That Is. They are the same. Your Eternal state is the reality and this human stage is the illusion through which you can choose to learn or return here as many times as needed before you ascend into the Divine Dimension.

Divine Light Beings, in formless states, in other dimensions, can be as aware of needs and challenges here, as are some of you in body. Divine Light Beings of all types continue their consciousness expansion just as you do, in other dimensions. God however is constant, pure love and light never changing from this constancy though always expanding in the constancy.

You are Divine Beings having a human experience. You are the Light of God and the hands and feet of the Oneness in this dimension. You are made in the image of God and you have come to both learn more about your Oneness and to heal as you are so called.

You are most effective when you call forth healing from knowing at your Core or at your Eternal Soul level. You are a Divine Being yourself. Any deep desire to heal when actualized by your free will, will be received by Divine Light Beings with unparalleled support and wisdom. Therefore, working in conscious Partnership with Divine Beings is a wonderful way to work while being in these temporary, limited human bodies. When you put together your call for Spiritual healing with those of the Divine realm, who carry this same desire for you, you access enhanced reality options for yourself. Together, you can manifest Wholeness and Love in this dimension.

To effectively call in Global Healing, we need to call forth the same number of human beings of Light from this dimension and Divine Beings from the Divine Realms to work together and focus on issues of healing in this dimension. This lesson in this lifetime was first taught to me when working with Hurricane Irene in 2011. You can read more about this experience by going to the following link on my website:

http://www.robbinshopkins.com/sermons/authentic-prayer-and-global-healing/

After heartfelt efforts to work with a few other humans to stem the potential disastrous effects of this hurricane, I was given a vision that led me to understand that I needed to vastly expand the pool of those working on this issue. Specifically, equal numbers of human beings and Divine Beings needed to come together to transform the hurricane energy. This partnering occurred and the force of the hurricane was greatly diminished. Undoubtedly many others were praying for this as well. This way to structure effective global healing experiences has been given over and over again while working on a range of global issues.

## GLOBAL CLEARING FOR NEGATIVE SPIRITS

One area that I have focused on globally for the past eight years has been the clearing of negative spirits from this dimension. Negative spirits, as explained earlier, are those who have died and chosen to remain in this dimension for a range of reasons. The term "negative" is a blanket term ranging in meaning from those who are unknowingly stuck here, to those who willingly remain and create mischief and havoc in this dimension. These spirits may be concerned about a family member, carry deep regret and guilt, be afraid of going to the Light, be angry, vengeful, committed to self-destruction, or any number of other reasons. They may simply have not had a ceremony that sent them to the Light with Divine help, so they missed the cues that others might have helped them to see.

However, all negative or stuck spirits need to be sent to the Light. They have no future here and they essentially stop growing and learning, as this is not their designated place to be. In other words, their choice to remain here has major consequences for themselves as well as for those of us in body. Their unhealed energy from their most recent lifetime is draining for any humans or animals they are around. Further, negative spirits without bodies cannot process the challenges from their former lives. This processing from previous lives needs to take place with Divine support in other dimensions. Their time to process and heal themselves from their previous or latest lifetime while in this dimension, ended when they passed out of their body.

In all cases, negative spirits need to go to the Light. Thus, global healing can be directly affected by helping spirits leave this dimension and return to the Oneness. I began this work with ones and twos, sending spirits into the Light. For several years, I have now worked with thousands of beings from specific countries and locations, pass into the Light. My work with negative spirits has always been done in partnership with the Angelic Host. The angels surround the individuals with Divine Light, to help them follow the Light.

There are a number of folks who have also been called to this work who have worked with me as they developed their skills. If called to work with large numbers of negative spirits stuck in this dimension, refer to the section on Casting Multiple Spirits to the Light in Chapter Eleven. Substitute the number of spirits who are potentially ready to leave this dimension in place of working with a single or a few spirits going to the Light. The processes are the same.

## SENDING OUT GLOBAL HEALING ENERGY

Another powerful type of global healing can occur through sending out specific healing energies around the globe to any humans in need, after a human being has received that healing in this dimension. After a specific healing vibration has been received in this dimension, all beings open and in need of that healing energy may receive it as well. This is a little known and infrequently used spiritual truth about healing.

All spiritual healing needs to be called forth while consciously working in Sacred Space. All healing protocols in this book focus on working in partnership with Divine Beings who bring varying gifts and talents from diverse backgrounds to support our growth and healing. One of the many reasons for working in partnership is because these Divine Entities can ensure global healing is received, if three conditions exist.

The first condition is that we are working in partnership with Divine Entities in a healing partnership. The second condition is that a specific set of Divine healing energies has been received by at least one human being in this dimension. The third is that those calling for healing for a specific person, also call for these healing vibrations to be made available to all persons needed this same healing support that day.

I was recently reminded of this most important act through my meditation groups. For several weeks, we had had low attendance and at one gathering I mused out loud that perhaps we should possibly consider disbanding our gatherings due to low attendance. The moment I closed my eyes in meditation I had the strong intuitive knowing that I was not looking at the larger picture regarding these meditation gatherings. These gatherings needed to continue as long as two or more were gathered because there was a huge support group that joined us of both Divine Beings and the spirits of human Light workers. Human Light workers are people who have come to Earth and agreed to work with the Divine Light while being in human body. Their spirits can work on a number of issues while being in body. Such a combination of Divine Beings and human Light worker spirits can make all received healing vibrations available for any others in need around the globe. The key is to have both human Light workers and Divine Eternal Being working together. We are not just doing this work for ourselves or for those whom we know. Any time healing is received in this dimension in any way, that possibility exists for all people as well.

I began to ask how many human beings were receiving healing on certain days and there were often many thousands indicated just from the work in our seemingly "small" meditation groups. I knew that we needed equal numbers of human Light workers and Divine Beings on both sides to work effectively together. I began to realize that we were in the presence of an indeterminate number of Divine Beings when we gathered to meditate. I had however not fully realized that by gathering in a small group, we could still affect large changes because the other needed numbers of human Light workers were joining us in spirit form while this healing energy was taking place. The combination of Divine and human Light workers in equal number is a very important ingredient in sending out healing vibrations to those in need.

Recently in my gathering space, five human beings gathered for meditation. Several hundred thousand Divine Beings joined us. Half were from the Divine realm and half were in the energetic form of human Light workers. When we began our first global healing prayers, we were joined by a couple of hundred Divine Beings. Each week, I would ask about numbers of Divine Beings working with us, and the numbers consistently expanded.

We open Sacred Space with a range of different types of Divine Beings. Those Beings tap into the Divine Light of human Light workers when a call for global healing is made. This happens because there are already numbers of Divine Light workers in body at any given time who have already given their eternal permission for their Light to be used for any healing purposes in this dimension.

This Partnership of human Light workers and Divine Beings can be reproduced by any meditation and healing group committed to the healing of the Greater Whole. We did not set out to expand our numbers of Divine Beings and human Light workers working with us. We began by listening to the guidance given within our Sacred Healing and Wisdom Circle for the areas needing rebalancing and healing in our dimension. We called for healing for ourselves, for those we knew and for conditions and situations that needed healing in this dimension as well. Each person received different guidance and direction about what needed to be focused upon. All else was given.

Our process is to have this global healing take place after we have opened our hearts and minds in conscious Sacred Space. We open to

Divine Source through shared spiritual readings, shared music, and group chanting. We then move to global prayer and each person speaks aloud softly as guided calling in Divine Transformational Light. We call for healing with individuals, groups, situations, and conditions as guided by our Divine Partners working with us, and by our own personal concerns for the healing of others in this dimension. It is Divine Partnership that brings forth the healing grace and transformational energy.

## WORKING WITH NATURE INTELLIGENCES

Another way to strengthen global healing efforts is to enlist the Nature Intelligences in the work being undertaken. During my first experience of working with Nature Intelligences, a colleague encouraged me to listen for messages from the sea creatures. I did not really know what this meant.

However, I found myself on the water front about 140 miles from the epicenter of the devastating 2010 earthquake in Haiti. Just after the earthquake shocks subsided, I listened deeply for how to help. I got the information that I needed to be patient while the intelligence from the sea was being translated so that I could hear it. I waited for nearly 20 minutes in Sacred Silence and finally I got, "we want to work with you to help with healing the waters around this island." I agreed to call in their loving energy, partnering with them and Divine Healing Entities as best I could.

I knew the communication came from the whales in that vicinity. That turned out to be essential in the quelling of potential tsunamis that would have ordinarily followed after such an earthquake. I saw in my mind's eye, groups of sea animals working together with the energy of the water supported by our gathering of human Light worker spirits and Divine Beings, to calm the seas around the Island of Haiti and the Dominican Republic. It was an extraordinary experience and I am sure I only understood just a very little bit of what was actually accomplished at that time to help bring balance.

Another example of this type of global healing occurred in France. I was working on the global level with issues of racism, terrorism, domestic violence, and financial stability. I was sitting at nearly 10,000 feet near Mont Blanc one day, when I was led to open healing space for this work. There were a range of old blocked stagnant energies including; fears and prejudice, financial improprieties, old thought patterns, violence, rage, etc. called forth for healing for that country and area.

It was very clear that this work was to be done at this high elevation over the country. I asked why this was occurring at such an altitude. I got that that high up, the air was pure and that the deep power of the mountains was participating in this healing with our group of human Light worker spirits and Divine Spirits. The energy was like none other I have ever worked with. The partnering energy was offered by the mountains themselves, joining with us for healing.

There are Nature Intelligences of all kinds. There are wind, air, fire, ether and water Intelligences. There are plant, mountain, ocean, animals, and sea creature Intelligences. There are tree, flower, earth, and lake Intelligences. There are fairy, invisible creature, and insect Intelligences. There are many others I have yet to meet as well. We can work with all these Intelligences in partnership with humans and Divine Beings to bring about greater peace, healing, and balance to our globe. We simply have to ask for the Nature Intelligence energy to join our Sacred Healing and Wisdom Circle. Again, we have to ask for what we need because we are Beings with free will and only when we ask, can the help we seek be given.

Machaelle Small Wright's *Behaving as if God in all Life Mattered* is an excellent resource for going more deeply into working with Nature Intelligences and Devas. This and other books can be found in the Further Reading and Resources section at the end of this book.

# AFTERWORD

May this book encourage you to expand your experiences in meditation, in working with Divine Beings, and in calling in healing for yourself and others. We are always heard. We are all completely wired for connection with Divine Presence by whatever name we use to speak of this Presence. The approaches offered here do work.

As we are each Divine Beings in human bodies, you will undoubtedly be led to other ways for calling forth healing as well. Use the approaches shared here to get you launched. As other information and different ways are given to access Divine Source, explore, refine, and share all that comes to you regarding healing energies and modalities.

All those called to do this work have come already primed to contribute to healing and wholeness in this dimension. May your learning and work be fully blessed as you continue to seek ways that will clear imbalances, ground that which is not grounded, heal the darkness, expand the Light, and increase the energy of Wholeness on this planet.

# APPENDIX

# Obesity, Anxiety, Abuse, Addiction

THERE ARE FOUR MAJOR IMBALANCES addressed here that affect millions of humans. These imbalances manifest as obesity, anxiety, abuse, and addiction trauma energies. Each of these manifestations affects millions of individuals, those with the imbalances themselves, along with their families, friends, and loved ones. Getting to all the underlying specific trauma energies related to these four major imbalances is a challenge. The lists in this chapter can help you get started with healing these areas if you or someone you know is manifesting these specific trauma energies.

## OBESITY TRAUMA ENERGY

The following appropriate trauma energies should be cleared at all levels of consciousness for anyone dealing with obesity trauma energy or chronic overweight issues. Use the Six-Step Spiritual Healing Protocol process and first clear for obesity trauma energy and all symptoms. Next clear these individual trauma energies "and all symptoms including obesity trauma energy." Each of these listed trauma energies has obesity trauma energy as one of the range of symptoms. This could take weeks or months to clear all of these areas of imbalance. Each time there is clearing, the individual moves closer to changing their relationship with weight imbalances.

- Excess weight trauma energy and all symptoms (including obesity trauma energy)
- Holding onto excess fat trauma energy and all symptoms
- Being out of Right Relationship with food trauma energy and all symptoms
- Self-protection trauma energy and all symptoms

- Self-loathing trauma energy and all symptoms
- Image trauma energy and all symptoms
- Body hatred trauma energy and all symptoms
- Feeling like a failure trauma energy and all symptoms
- Desire to feel satisfied trauma energy and all symptoms
- Desire to feel safe trauma energy and all symptoms
- Overeating trauma energy and all symptoms
- Feeling hopeless trauma energy and all symptoms
- Microbial trauma energy and all symptoms
- Sugar dependence trauma energy and all symptoms
- Desire to feel loved trauma energy and all symptoms including overeating
- Negative expectations trauma energy and all symptoms
- Starving trauma energy and all symptoms
- Desire to feel in control trauma energy and all symptoms
- Gene-induced excess weight trauma energy and all symptoms for the entire genetic line (Determine from Divine Source, the specific number of genes involved, if possible.)
- Food obsession trauma energy and all symptoms
- Abuse trauma energy and all symptoms (including obesity, sexual, physical, emotional, mental imbalances)
- Bullying trauma energy and all symptoms
- Abandonment trauma energy and all symptoms
- Unwanted child trauma energy and all symptoms

## ANXIETY TRAUMA ENERGY

The following appropriate trauma energies should be cleared for all levels of consciousness for anyone dealing with anxiety trauma energy and all symptoms. Use the Six-Step Spiritual Healing Protocol process and first clear for anxiety trauma energy and all symptoms. Next clear these individual trauma energies "and all symptoms including anxiety trauma energy." Each of these listed trauma energies has anxiety trauma energy as one of the range of symptoms. This could take weeks or months to clear all of these areas of imbalance. Each time there is clearing, the individual moves closer to changing their relationship with anxiety.

- Feeling vulnerable trauma energy and all symptoms (including anxiety trauma energy)
- Fear of being overwhelmed trauma energy and all symptoms
- Fear of falling apart trauma energy and all symptoms
- Fear of failing trauma energy and all symptoms
- Familial abuse trauma energy and all symptoms (father, mother, sibling, uncle, grandfather, etc.)
- Trusted adult (name person or role) abuse trauma energy and all symptoms
- Feeling unsafe trauma energy and all symptoms
- Feeling unloved trauma energy and all symptoms
- Feeling unwanted trauma energy and all symptoms
- Genocide trauma (Holocaust) trauma energy and all symptoms
- Solitary confinement trauma energy and all symptoms
- Violence trauma energy and all symptoms
- Fear of being in body trauma energy and all symptoms
- Panic attack trauma energy and all symptoms
- Self-criticism trauma energy and all symptoms
- Blame trauma energy and all symptoms
- Shame trauma energy and all symptoms
- Perfection trauma energy and all symptoms
- Fear of failing in one's life purpose trauma energy and all symptoms
- Fear of judgment trauma energy and all symptoms
- Self-loathing trauma energy and all symptoms
- Fear of others' opinions trauma energy and all symptoms
- Gene-induced anxiety trauma energy and all symptoms for the entire genetic line (The specific number of genes involved is helpful to determine from Divine Source.)
- Betrayal trauma energy and all symptoms
- Abandonment trauma energy and all symptoms
- Negative spirit presence trauma energy and all symptoms
- Fear of navigating in public trauma energy and all symptoms
- Fear of being criticized and all symptoms
- Fear of being found lacking trauma energy and all symptoms
- Loss of one's purpose in life trauma energy and all symptoms

- Loss of one's partner (or child, spouse, parent, sibling, friend, animal, home, job, memory, etc.) trauma energy and all symptoms

## ABUSE TRAUMA ENERGY

The following appropriate trauma energies should be cleared for all levels of consciousness for anyone dealing with abuse trauma energy and all symptoms. Use the Six-Step Spiritual Healing Protocol process and first clear for abuse trauma energy and all symptoms. Next clear these individual trauma energies "and all symptoms including abuse trauma energy." Each of these listed trauma energies has abuse trauma energy as one of the symptoms. This could take weeks or months to clear all of these areas of imbalance. Each time there is clearing, the individual moves closer to changing their relationship with abuse.

- Self-condemnation trauma energy and all symptoms (including abuse trauma energy).
- Childhood trauma energy and all symptoms
- Self-denigration trauma energy and all symptoms
- Victim behavior trauma energy and all symptoms
- Feeling vulnerable trauma energy and all symptoms
- Feeling afraid trauma energy and all symptoms
- Feeling inferior trauma energy and all symptoms
- Feeling damaged trauma energy and all symptoms
- Shock trauma energy and all symptoms
- Rage trauma energy and all symptoms
- Feeling disconnected from Divine Source trauma energy and all symptoms
- Physical violence trauma energy and all symptoms
- Emotional violence trauma energy and all symptoms
- Mental violence trauma energy and all symptoms
- Being raped trauma energy and all symptoms
- Pornography trauma energy and all symptoms
- Blame trauma energy and all symptoms
- Abandonment (by God, parent, sibling, etc.) trauma energy and all symptoms
- Self-cutting trauma energy trauma energy and all symptoms

- Self-harming trauma energy and all symptoms
- Self-hatred trauma energy and all symptoms
- Body-hatred trauma energy and all symptoms
- Hiding from life trauma energy and all symptoms
- Failure to thrive trauma energy and all symptoms
- Failure to bond trauma energy and all symptoms
- Fear of never healing trauma energy and all symptoms
- Trust trauma energy and all symptoms
- Go it alone trauma energy and all symptoms
- Numbing behavior (e.g. over-drinking, taking illegal drugs, over-sleeping, etc.) trauma energy and all symptoms
- Bulimia trauma energy and all symptoms
- Anorexia trauma energy and all symptoms
- Carrying the past trauma energy and all symptoms
- Failure expectations trauma energy and all symptoms
- Negative expectation trauma energy and all symptoms
- Chakra trauma energy and all symptoms
- Ungrounded trauma energy and all symptoms
- Kleptomania trauma energy and all symptoms
- Credit card debt trauma energy and all symptoms
- Alcohol trauma energy and all symptoms
- Lying trauma energy and all symptoms
- Manipulation trauma energy and all symptoms
- Narcissism trauma energy and all symptoms
- Extortion trauma energy and all symptoms
- Fraud trauma energy and all symptoms

## ADDICTION TRAUMA ENERGY

The following appropriate trauma energies should be cleared for all levels of consciousness for anyone dealing with addiction trauma energy and all symptoms. Use the Six-Step Spiritual Healing Protocol process and first clear for addiction trauma energy and all symptoms. Next clear these individual trauma energies "and all symptoms including addiction trauma energy". Each of these listed trauma energies has addiction trauma energy as one of the symptoms. This could take weeks or months to clear all of these areas of imbalance. Each time there is clearing, the individual moves closer to changing their relationship with addiction.

- Familial (or father, mother, sibling, uncle, grandfather, etc.) abuse trauma energy and all symptoms (including addiction trauma energy)
- Trusted adult [name person or role] abuse trauma energy and all symptoms
- Physical violence trauma energy and all symptoms
- Emotional violence trauma energy and all symptoms
- Mental violence trauma energy and all symptoms
- Self-hatred trauma energy and all symptoms
- Self-condemnation trauma energy and all symptoms
- Gene-induced addiction trauma energy and all symptoms for the entire genetic line (Determine from Divine Source, the specific number of genes involved, if possible.)
- Failure trauma energy and all symptoms
- Victim trauma energy and all symptoms
- Rage trauma energy and all symptoms
- Bully trauma energy and all symptoms
- Belittling trauma energy and all symptoms
- Judgment trauma energy and all symptoms
- Loss of hope trauma energy and all symptoms
- Want to die trauma energy and all symptoms
- Thrill seeking trauma energy and all symptoms
- Self-gratification trauma energy and all symptoms
- Narcissism trauma energy and all symptoms
- Nothing to lose trauma energy and all symptoms
- Impervious to others trauma energy and all symptoms
- Seeking continuous highs trauma energy and all symptoms
- No way out belief trauma energy and all symptoms
- Feeling disconnected from Divine Source trauma energy and all symptoms
- Desire to die trauma energy and all symptoms
- Cynicism trauma energy and all symptoms
- Nothing I do matters trauma energy and all symptoms

- Life sucks trauma energy and all symptoms
- Loser trauma energy and all symptoms
- Negative self-judgment trauma energy and all symptoms
- Seeking numbing behavior trauma energy and all symptoms
- Feeling unsafe trauma energy and all symptoms
- Feeling alone trauma energy and all symptoms

# THE SIX-STEP SPIRITUAL HEALING PROTOCOL

## 1. Open Sacred Space

*I open this Sacred Healing and Wisdom Circle and invite my I AM Energy to be present. I welcome the Angelic Host, the Ascended Masters, the Cosmic Light Beings of the Universe, the Devas and Nature Intelligences, and the Divine Healing Entities of the Highest Light from all traditions to partner with me in our shared knowing of the Oneness.*

## 2. Prepare and Listen

*I open my heart, mind, body, affairs, relationships and soul to Divine Presence to receive all that is available for me in this healing work today. I clear for the blocked energies of doubt and hesitation to call forth healing; for bias, preference, and attachment to specific desired outcomes; and for un-forgiveness of my self and others. I am listening and know ALL things are possible.*

## 3. Name the Imbalance

*My imbalance is [name of imbalance] trauma energy and all symptoms.*

EXAMPLES OF IMBALANCES: Guilt, abuse, pride, lying, unfaithfulness, fear of being out of Right Relationship with [person or situation], blame, resentment, death, fear, accident, loss, despondency, grief, shame, cancer, sciatic nerve imbalance, low back pain, insomnia, loneliness, judgment, impatience with self and life, apathy, addiction, abandonment, betrayal, rage, depression, etc.

## 4. Command Out and Clear Blocked Energies

*I call forth the Sacred Flame (or Divine Source, the Great I AM energy, My Divine Self, Eternal Flame, the Oneness the Christ energy) within me.*

*Sacred Flame, clear continuously all blocked emotional, mental, thermal, spiritual, hereditary line, karmic, curse, and spell energies back through all time and space from all lifetimes and originating sources, from all memories and patterns and down to the cells in my body manifesting as [name of imbalance] trauma energy and all symptoms.*

*Consume all blocked energies at the conscious, subconscious, unconscious, and supra-conscious levels contributing in any way to [name of imbalance] trauma energy and all symptoms.*

## 5. Maximize the Healing

*I call forth the appropriate Divine Healing Entities and the Angels to bring all needed Divine vibrational intervention healing at the physical level due to [name of imbalance] trauma energy and all symptoms at the highest possible rate of healing. I call forth Divine Stellar healing.*

*I am totally worthy of healing (or another affirmation).*

EXAMPLES OF AFFIRMATIONS: I am the Peace I seek. I am Perfect Love Energy. I am Light everlasting. I am Perfect Love in body. I am Capable and Loveable. Everything that is needed is provided. I am Eternal. I Am One with All That Is. I have all the chances I need to heal. I co-create with Divine Source. I respond to life in the present moment. I <u>love myself</u> (forgive myself, open to Divine Source, etc.) wholly and completely. I am the Healing Light I seek. I am <u>patience</u> (compassion, ease and grace, forgiveness, etc.) personified.

## 6. Close the Sacred Space

*With Divine partnership, we send these healing energies around the globe, to all those who can receive them this day.*

*I offer my deep appreciation to all Divine Beings carrying healing vibrations throughout this dimension to those who can receive them today. I give my profound thanks to the Sacred Healing and Wisdom Circle partners for their support and healing wisdom. I am so deeply blessed. My thanks. All this healing is manifesting in Divine Order. And So It is. Amen.*

www.robbinshopkins.com

# ACKNOWLEDGEMENTS

I want to acknowledge my extraordinary clients and fellow meditators from whom I have had the chance to learn deeply about spiritual healing and wholeness.

I am profoundly grateful, Giles, for your reading my many drafts, offering your cogent comments, patiently working with me on the formatting, and organization of this book. Your incredible support and insights have strengthened this book immeasurably.

My lasting thanks to Teague, Leah, and Devon for your suggestions about this book, your exploration and openness about spiritual growth, and your loving support of me.

Thank you, Nettie, for your extensive work on my book draft and for our shared spiritual seeking in India and Brazil. I am so appreciative of all I have learned from you about the unknown.

Thank you, Trey, for the super cover design, the graphics for the book, and for your wonderful energy in working with me. I send thanks to the team at Balboa Press for expert assistance at every step of the process.

For the years of spiritual journeying together, I thank all those in my meditation groups (you know who you are) from whom I learn weekly. I offer my thanks to Kathy, Susi, Carole, Annie, Terri, Gail, Bruce, and Theresa for all we have spiritually sought and learned together. My additional thanks to Pat for reading my draft, sharing your insights and suggestions.

My love and thanks to you, Thomas, for trusting me to work with you through tough times and for always being open to a spiritual dialogue. My appreciation to all my family members who have shown an interest in my spiritual learning and my healing practice.

I thank all my wonderful yoga teachers for their loving instruction, especially Greg, Stephanie and Cynthia who have helped me live yoga in deeply spiritual and delightful ways.

I thank my Divine Book Team Partners who listened to all the reasons I could not write this book, over and over again, and still were always available to work with me on getting this information out into the world.

I have had some wonderful teachers and mentors along my journey. My thanks to Ron Roth who introduced me to spiritual healing in action, who inspired my seminary work, and championed an interfaith view of the world.

My thanks to Harrison Owen for introducing me to Open Space, which is spiritual gathering in action. I give thanks to Angeles Arrien for leading three profound workshops at a formative time in my life and for introducing me to drumming, storytelling, and totem animals. I offer my thanks to David Hawkins who inspired my every step to greater consciousness through his books and workshops.

I offer my thanks to the many hundreds of thousands of Divine Beings who have worked with me for lifetimes and continue to work with me today. Most notably in this time I thank Babaji, Buddha, Jesus, Lao-Tzu, Divine Mother, Archangels Michael, Metatron, Raphael, Gabriel, Chamuel, and Auriel, Saint Germain, Yogananda, Yuketeswar, Shirdi Sai Baba, Master Kuthumi, Sri Aurobindo, Sai Baba, and Carl Jung.

I am incredibly grateful and blessed that all these magnificent loved ones and sojourners have been my teachers every step of my journey.

I offer my profound appreciation to all of you, from the bottom of my heart.

# ENDNOTES

1    David R. Hawkins, *Power vs. Force; The Hidden Determinants of Human Behavior*, Carlsbad, California: Hay House, Inc., 2006.

2    Deepak Chopra, *Creating Affluence: The A-to-Z Steps to a Richer Life*, San Rafael, California: Amber-Allen Publishing, 1998, Kindle Edition, Chapter 4, page 1.

3    Ibid, Chapter 4, page 2.

4    Angeles Arrien, *Four Fold Way: Walking the Paths of the Warrior, Teacher, Healer, and Visionary*, San Francisco, California: Harper, 1993.

5    Emmet Fox, from "The Golden Gate" in *Power Through Constructive Thinking*, San Francisco, California: Harper Collins, 1989, page 267

6    David R. Hawkins, page 2.

7    Ibid., pages 2, 295.

8    Saint Germain Foundation, *The I AM Discourses*, Schaumberg, Illinois: Saint Germain Press, 1940.

9    Sagan, Carl, Ann Druyan, Steven Soter, Adrian Malone, Tom Weidlinger, Geoffrey Haines-Stiles, David Kennard, et al. *Cosmos: A Personal Voyage*, Studio City, CA: Cosmos Studios, 2000

10   *A Course in Miracles*, Glen Ellen, CA: Foundation for Inner Peace, 1992, page 84.

11   Gary Renard, *Disappearance of the Universe: Straight Talk about Illusions, Past Lives, Religion, Sex, Politics, and the Miracles of Forgiveness*, Carlsbad, California: Hay House, Inc., 2004, page 124.

12   BBC Horizon, producer, *Ghost in Our Genes* aired on PBS, NOVA October 16, 2007 companion website url http:// www.bbc.co.uk/sn/tvradio/programmes/horizen/ghostgenes.shtml (accessed November 17, 2016).

13   BioethicsBytes, *Epigenetics – The ghost in your genes*, June 30, 2008 https://bioethicsbytes.wordpress.com/2008/06/30/ epigenetics-the-ghost-in-your-genes/ accessed November 17, 2016.

14   Joe Vitale, *Zero Limits*

15   Frank Lobsiger, *The Art of Selflove*, Estavayer-Le-Lac, Switzerland: AraKara Publication, 2010.

16   Ibid., page 76.

17   Ibid., page 76.

# FURTHER READING AND RESOURCES

Arrien, Angeles, *Four Fold Way: Walking the Paths of the Warrior, Teacher, Healer, and Visionary*, San Francisco, California: Harper, 1993.

Chapman, Gary, The 5 Love Languages: The Secret to Love That Lasts, Chicago, Illinois: Northfield Publishing, 1984.

Chopra, Deepak, *Creating Affluence: The A-to-Z Steps to a Richer Life*, San Rafael, California: Amber-Allen Publishing, 1998.

Chopra, Deepak, *The Third Jesus: The Christ We Cannot Ignore*, New York, New York: Three Rivers Press, 2008.

Cockell, Jenny, *Across Time and Death: A Mother's Search for Her Past Life Children*, New York, New York: Simon & Schuster, 1993.

Dyer, Wayne W., *There's A Spiritual Solution to Every Problem*, New York, New York: Harper Collins, 2001.

Emoto, Masaru, *The Hidden Messages in Water*, Hillsboro, Oregon: Beyond Words Publishing, 2004.

Faulds, Donna, *Limitless: New Poems and Other Writings*, Greenville, Virginia: Peaceable Kingdom Books, 2009.

Faulds, Donna, *Breath of Joy: Poems, Prayers, and Prose*, Kearney, Nebraska: Morris Publishing, *2013*.

Fox, Emmet, *Make Your Life Worthwhile*, New York, New York: Harper Collins, 1946.

Fox, Emmet, *Power Through Constructive Thinking*, San Francisco, California: Harper Collins, 1989.

Goldsmith, Joel S., *The Foundation of Mysticism: Spiritual Healing Principles of the Infinite Way*, Lakewood, Colorado: Acropolis Books, 1998.

Goldsmith, Joel S., *A Message for the Ages*, Atlanta, Georgia: Acropolis Books, 2002.

Goldsmith, Joel S., *The Art of Spiritual Living*, Atlanta, Georgia: Acropolis Books, 2002.

Hawkins, David R., *The Eye of the I*, West Sedona, Arizona: Veritas Publishing, 2001.

Hawkins, David R., *Power vs. Force; The Hidden Determinants of Human Behavior*, Carlsbad, California: Hay House, Inc., 2006.

Hawkins, David R., *Transcending the Levels of Consciousness: The Stairway to Enlightenment*, West Sedona, Arizona: Veritas Publishing, 2006.

Hay, Louise, *You Can Heal Your Life*, Carlsbad, California: Hay House, Inc., 1999.

Hodge, Stephen with Boord, Martin, *The Illustrated Tibetan Book of he Dead*, New York, New York: Sterling Publishing Company, Inc., 1999.

Huber, Cheri, *Nothing Happens Next: Responses to Questions About Meditation*, Keep It Simple Books, 1995.

Huber, Cheri, *Suffering Is Optional*, Keep It Simple Books, 2000.

Ingerman, Sandra, *Soul Retrieval: Mending the Fragmented Self*, San Francisco, California: Harper Collins Publishers, 1991.

Kabat-Zinn, Jon, *Wherever You Go, There You Are*, New York, New York: Hyperion, 1994.

Keating, Thomas, *Open Mind, Open Heart: The Contemplative Dimension of the Gospel*, New York, New York: Continuum International Publishing Group, 1994.

Lao-Tzu and John C. H. Wu, *Tao Teh Ching*, New York, New York: St. John's University Press, 1961.

Lobsiger, Frank, *The Art of Selflove*, Estavayer-Le-Lac, Switzerland: AraKara Publication, 2010.

Morgan, Marlo, *Mutant Message Downunder*, Lees Summit, Missouri: MM Co., 1991.

Myss, Caroline, *Anatomy of the Spirit*, New York, New York: Harmony Books, 1997.

Nhăt Hanh, Thích, *Living Buddha, Living Christ*, New York, New York: Penguin Group, 1995.

Newton, Michael, *Journey of Souls, Case Studies of Life Between Lives*, Woodbury, Minnesota: Llewellyn Publications, 2010.

Owen, Harrison, *The Power of Spirit: How To Transform Organizations*, San Francisco, California: Barrett-Koehler Publishers, Inc., 2000.

Pierrakos, Eva and Thesenga, Donovan, *Fear No Evil: The Pathwork Method of Transforming The Lower Self*, Madison, Virginia: Pathwork Press, 1993.

Renard, Gary R., *The Disappearance of the Universe: Straight Talk about Illusions, Past Lives, Religion, Sex, Politics, and the Miracles of Forgiveness*, Carlsbad, California: Hay House, Inc., 2004.

Rodegast, Pat and Stanton, Judith, *Emmanuel's Book II: The Choice for Love*, New York, New York: Bantam Books, 1989.

Roth, Ron, and Occhiogrosso, Peter, *Healing Path of Prayer: A Modern Mystic's Guide to Spiritual Power*, New York, New York: Three Rivers Press, 1977.

Roth, Ron, and Occhiogrosso, Peter, *Prayer and the Five Stages of Healing*, Carlsbad, California: Hay House, Inc., 1999.

Saint Germain Foundation, *The I AM Discourses, Volumes 3 and 15*, Schaumberg, Illinois: Saint Germain Press, 1940.

Sanford, Agnes, *The Healing Light*, New York, New York: Ballantine Books, 1972.

Szekely, Edmond Bordeaux (ed.), *The Essene Gospel of Peace: Book One*, International Biogenic Society, 1981.

Takyi, H.K., and Khubchandani, Kishin J., *Words of Jesus and Sathya Sai Baba*, Puni, India: Kishin J. Khubchandani, 1998.

Tolle, Eckhart, *A New Earth*, New York, New York: Penguin Group, 2005.

Tolle, Eckhart, *The Power of Now: A Guide to Spiritual Enlightenment*, Navato, California: Namaste Publishing and New World Library, 1997.

Vaughan, Frances and Walsh, Roger, *Accept This Gift: Selections from A Course in Miracles*, New York, New York: Penguin Group, 1983.

Vaughan, Frances and Walsh, Roger, *Gifts from a Course in Miracles: Accept This Gift, A Gift of Peace, A Gift of Healing*, New York, New York: Penguin Putnam, Inc., 1988.

Virtue, Doreen, *Divine Prescriptions: Using Your Sixth Sense – Spiritual Solutions for You and Your Loved Ones*, Los Angeles, California: Renaissance Books, 2000.

Vitale, Joe and Hew Len, Ihaleakala, *Zero Limits: The Secret Hawaiian System for Wealth, Health, Peace, and More*, Hoboken, New Jersey: John Wiley and Sons, 2007.

Walsh, Neale Donald, *Conversations with God: An Uncommon Dialogue*, New York, New York: G.P. Putnam's Sons, 1995.

Weiss, Brian L., *Many Lives, Many Masters: The True Story of a Prominent Psychiatrist, His Young Patient, and the Past-Life Therapy That Changed Both Their Lives*, New York, New York: Simon & Schuster, 1988.

Weiss, Brian L., *Same Soul, Many Bodies: Discover the Healing Power of Future Lives through Progression Therapy*, New York, New York: Free Press of Simon & Schuster, 2005.

William, Anthony, *Medical Medium: Secrets Behind Chronic and Mystery Illness and How to Finally Heal*, Carlsbad, California: Hay House, Inc. 2015.

Wright, Machaelle Small, *Behaving As If God in All Life Mattered*, Warrenton, Virginia: Perelandra, Ltd., 1997.

Wright, Machaelle Small, *Dancing in the Shadows of the Moon,* Warrenton, Virginia: Perelandra, Ltd., 1995.

Yogananda, Paramahansa, *Autobiography of a Yogi*, Los Angeles, California: Self-Realization Fellowship, 1998.

Yogananda, Paramahansa, *In the Sanctuary of the Soul*, Los Angeles, California: Self-Realization Fellowship, 1998.

# ABOUT THE AUTHOR

Robbins Hopkins was raised in the segregated south of the US and moved at age thirteen with her family to The Netherlands. This experience profoundly re-shaped her views of equality, justice, tolerance, acceptance, and suffering. Her continued interest in cross-cultural communications led her to a career in global exchange program management and research.

She earned a Masters and Doctorate in intercultural communications and counseling. She then co-founded a management consulting firm and specialized in team building for multicultural teams engaged in global, economic, and social development.

Throughout her life, Robbins has made spiritual pilgrimages to Mexico, India, Brazil, Spain, France, and the Southwestern United States to work with spiritual leaders and healers. She eventually sought a deeper connection with Divine Source and became an ordained interfaith minister specializing in spiritual healing. She spent seven years in intensive Spirit-led silent meditation and inner healing to develop the basis for her spiritual healing and guidance practice.

Drawing on 44 years of leading workshops, developing training materials, and international consulting, Robbins now mentors a community of spiritual meditators and healers. Working with Divine Partnerships, she provides in-person, long-distance, and global spiritual healing.

Robbins loves hiking, nature, and the beach. She enjoys finding balance through her daily gym workouts and yoga classes. She is married with two sons and a daughter-in-law. She has lived in suburban Washington, D.C. in an extended family household for 40 years.

Learn more at www.robbinshopkins.com.

Printed in the United States
By Bookmasters